Annette

be.come

the location
beneath the surface.

— WATER —
go below the water

March 2/17

Edited by: Kristin van Vloten, Chloe Sjuberg, Jennifer Chernecki, Barbara Swail, Sharilyn Hunter

Design and Layout by: Laura Reynolds, Studio TGP

Author Photograph by: Laura Reynolds, Studio TGP

Illustrations by: Jennifer Chernecki, Studio TGP

Publisher: Studio TGP   www.studiotgp.com

Author: www.trynagower.com

ISBN-10: 0995184607

ISBN-13: 978-0995184602

Printed in the United States of America

begin to be.

written through *Tryna Gower*

DEDICATION

This book is dedicated to the most important woman
in my life, my grandmother Adel Doris Spacil.
I love you.

~ Birdie ~

WORDS FOR TRYNA

"Tryna Spacil-Gower is a woman of profound beauty and magnitude. Written in a compelling and fresh voice, *be.come* is a guide for each of us to trust in our process of be.coming who we were born to be. Courage is our guide, and is clearly demonstrated and directed by the power of love. The love Tryna shared with her grandma taught her to trust her grandma's guidance from the afterlife, with every breath she took, here in the present. Through this wonderful journey, we are introduced to Tryna's unfolding life as a spirit medium, despite her ongoing resistance, and the gift we receive is the knowing that love has no ending; it is the eternal power and grace that resides within the essence of every one of us. This is a simple and beautiful book: two clear indicators that you are holding a true treasure within your hands."

— **Heather McCloskey-Beck**
Inspirational Speaker / Author / Founder of the Peace Flash Movement
www.heathermccloskeybeck.com

"Tryna is truly a remarkable force in that she has amazingly powerful abilities to motivate and inspire. I think of Tryna as a beacon… standing in her authenticity and sending out the message that it's okay for us to stand in our authenticity as well."

— **Ruby Tunke**
Spirit Writer / Author
www.rubytunke.com

CONTENTS

ACKNOWLEDGMENTS

This book was given to you, the reader, as a gift from my grandma and me. I want to thank some very key people that helped me create it and thank the special people who not only participated in my life but also stepped in as loyal, encouraging cheerleaders who wanted nothing but the best for me.

Taryn Tappen, my project manager, for showing up in my life and being the get-it-done girl. Without you, this would have never even been started. Laura Reynolds, my designer extraordinaire, the woman that keeps up to my ever-changing world and creates me beautiful works of art on demand, always. Jennifer Chernecki, my talented illustrator and details girl. Grandma set us up just in time to walk each other to the next phase. Without all three of you this book would never be.

My grandma always picks the best people for me. The most important phase of my life includes my Tribe of spiritually exploring friends. Approximately 20 beautiful ladies, all with energetic gifts of their own, are completely responsible for allowing me to grow and become how I am today. Without their friendships I would have never had the guts to share my stories and publish this book. In fear of missing a name, I send you all my deepest thanks and love for your roles in my life.

Finally, to my husband Brooks and children Tyler and Koby, for standing beside me through the hard parts of this process. Seeing me sitting at the computer for weeks on end, hair not brushed and emotionally riding a roller coaster, because that's how it really looks to write a book, at least for me. But I am thankful for each and every experience and relationship that has helped change my life for the better.

I love you all,

~Tryna~

preface

Preface

This is a book that I, Tryna Gower, technically wrote between 2014 and 2016. I say *technically* because although I was the one doing the typing, the bulk of this story was communicated to me by the spirit of my deceased Cree grandmother, Adel Doris Spacil.

To provide context for my grandma's message — a message she wants me to publicly share in the form of a book — I have placed it within my own story. A story of growing up in a mostly white family and feeling like an outsider. A story of culture loss and restoration. A story of abuse and brokenness — as well as healing and spiritual breakthrough.

The events I have recounted in this book are 100 per cent true. I have also recorded Grandma's words to me as faithfully as possible so that I could ensure I wasn't diluting or distorting her message.

It's my hope that by following my journey and absorbing Grandma's wisdom, you will experience the transformations I did. It's my wish that you, too, will learn to how to *be.come.*

And before you begin reading this story, Grandma has a few words to say:

Many will not understand the book at first but will eventually find their way to it because the universe is a bit behind the story. But it won't take long for them to cross over and join, in joy and love.

Be safe, be okay. Love. People will honour the process and take it in and many will re-read for years to come because they feel the word. Family will heal (including mine) and so many others will understand each other so much better as a result of the book. And you, Tryna, will *be.come* your best in the process.

May it be so,

adel D. Spacil

Adel D. Spacil

the end

chapter 1

conversations about the end...

Grandma died on March 27, 2010, at the age of 82 years old. Three years prior to her departure we had an unforgettable conversation. This is the story of that conversation, and the many unforgettable conversations that followed it.

Sometime in 2007, I am sitting on the old decrepit iron stackable chair with a thick heavily-stained floral cushion that Grandma purchased from the Sally Ann. I am facing her kitchen entrance. Grandma comes out of the hallway in her usual perfectly-pressed white silk blouse and navy blue slacks. At 79 years old, she is frail and has lost a lot of weight. Her hair is thin and white and you can almost see her entire scalp. She is barely able to walk without support as her legs have become weak from many years of sitting indoors cooking, cleaning, reading and sewing. When she comes around the corner her expression is disheartened and worried.

I look up into her small and wrinkled face. Her five-foot-tall body stops and stands right in front of me. She is cradling a cast-covered arm that was hurt in a fall caused by the mild stroke she suffered a couple of weeks ago while cooking in the kitchen. She knocked herself on the stove or cupboards and fell to the ground, breaking her frail arm instantly.

"Gram, what's the matter?" I ask. "You look sad."

"Birdie," she replies, using my childhood nickname. "I am scared to die."

Gathering my thoughts, taking a deep breath, and shifting my body, I try to hold it together emotionally. I hadn't been expecting such a bold statement to come out of her. I know

Chapter 1

be.come

this is big. This conversation needs to be handled with absolute delicacy and the greatest tact that I can muster. My nerves are vibrating, but I put on a strong front for her.

"Grandma, why are you so scared to die? I mean, really, we are all going to die one day, you know."

I try to use my voice in the most loving tone possible with just an edge of playfulness to lighten her fears. It is the best I can pull off at this moment. I have a reputation for being a sarcastic jokester among the members of my family, so I know I can get away with this. What other option do I have anyway? This conversation feels really strange and uncomfortable.

She appears to be deeply concerned, kind of checked out, and really sad. "I just don't know whether I am going up or down," she says, while she points her finger up to Heaven and then down to Hell to signal the severity of the topic.

"Oh, Gram, you are so going up!" I cheekily respond.

Chapter 1

"How do you know that?"

"Well, it's because you're Catholic, Grandma!"

Good one, I say to myself, giving myself an invisible pat on the back for my super-intelligent, quick response. I even surprised myself with that one!

"Aghhh," she snarls and walks off muttering in her native Cree tongue. "Do you really think so?" she asks, praying for some sign of hope.

Looking for a quick exit from this intense conversation, I finish it off with: "Heck yeah, of course! I mean, you go to church; you're a good girl, Gram. The big guy up there knows that," while pointing up to the heavens. I personally have never spent more than the occasional funeral or wedding in a church, so what would I know about the rules of God and church, Heaven or Hell? But my words seem to satisfy her temporarily. That is enough for me.

A few minutes later, she follows with: "How do you really know I am going to Heaven? What will it be like?"

Chapter 1
be.come

"Well, Gram, as you know, I haven't obviously been there yet, but from what I hear the place is pretty spectacular!"

Still trying to make some fun come alive in an uncomfortable situation, I continue with my perky attitude and witty comebacks. But I know I still haven't really helped Grandma feel better, and looking at her I can see that she's right. It's getting close to *that* time for her, all right. What can I do? Her situation is obvious and she knows it.

So I throw in my final slam-dunk move. "Grandma, I have an idea. Why don't we do an experiment? When you get to the other side, why don't you send me a signal to let me know you are there?"

"What?" she asks with a disbelieving and doubting face.

"How about this? When you get to the other side, why don't you mess with my pictures and I will know that it's really you?"

Scrunching her nose, she says, "Aghhhh, no, that's silly."

"For example," I say, "turn them over, tip them upside down, make them face backwards… just do anything weird with them and then I will know it's you!"

This idea comes to me out of nowhere. I am a professional photographer and most of my family members enjoy and appreciate the value of photographs. Grandma's walls are covered in them. I am surprised at my suggestion to her but I don't let her know this. Grandma flicks her hand in the air and walks away, appearing to have no interest in this idea at all. For some reason my instincts tell me to stay with this thought. Something about it feels weird, strange and significant. I file it away for a later date.

Approximately one year after our first initial Heaven/Hell conversation, Grandma's memory starts to slip. She is forever repeating her life stories over and over to anyone who will listen. Her comments about being afraid to die pop out again. So I pretend that I have never heard it before and repeat my response just as I did the first time.

This time she responds with: "Pictures? How on God's green earth do you think that will happen?"

Chapter 1
be.come

"Grandma, I honestly have no idea at all. But let's do this experiment. Let's try it, okay?" I am getting a little bit excited about it now for some weird reason. "If it's possible, then we get to do it together."

She kind of shrugs it off as weird yet again, but something inside of me says, "Stay with this." I know I need to complete my mission. I hope that I have enough time before the Creator takes her away from me to convince her to do this. Luckily, this scenario repeats itself one more time in the following year. She seems to be hearing me now. The mission, for the time being, feels completed.

On her final day on earth, March 26, 2010, Grandma lays in her bed. She is cranky and uncomfortable, with many people coming and going. I know I'm not going to get much time to be alone with her before she dies.

We are all pretending that everything is fine, making her believe that she is going to get better and get out of the hospital. We had been visiting, laughing and giving her

24-hour support while she rested in bed. Grandma is very uncomfortable. She isn't eating, can barely breathe, and keeps talking about getting the frog out of her throat. Her lungs are filling up with water and the nurses are giving us a heads-up that time is short.

On the inside I am so nervous. I have never witnessed anyone actually die before. What will it be like for me and for her? Other family members are sobbing and stressing when they leave the room, but although I am nervous, I don't actually feel like crying at all. I can't cry; I don't even have it in me. It surprises my dad. "You kids are so strong," he says, shaking his head.

Late into the evening in the hospital room on March 26, I notice Grandma raising her hands and arms very peacefully into the air. She makes fists with both hands. She seems to be punching the air ever so gently and her facial expression looks focused. I glance over to my dad who is seated on the other side of the hospital bed. I use my body language with a nod of the head to ask, "What is she doing?" He throws back an "I don't know" with large eyes and a shrug of his shoulders.

Chapter 1

be.come

"Grandma, what are you doing?" I gently ask. Because of her lung situation, she barely whispers out the word *"bannock."* "Bannock?" I repeat.

After a couple of seconds pondering the word, I realize what's happening. "Oh, Dad, she wants to actually teach us how to make bannock before she dies!"

"What are you talking about?" he asks with a very serious look on his face. He's emotional and stressed and knows that his mother will be leaving him very soon. He's in no mood for my sarcasm or any antics. I tell my dad that I always used to ask her to teach me how to make bannock so that I could have at least one native skill or hobby and we just never got around to it.

It appears she is ready to teach me.

the bannock recipe

chapter 2

how a heritage was lost…

Chapter 2
be.come

My grandma always knew that I was curious about my native heritage. I was the only child born of three that even looked like a native. Both of my native grandmothers married white men. My siblings turned out looking very white and I turned out looking much more like an Indian.

During my younger years, I was teased constantly for my native look and my sister and brother would constantly chant out, "You're the Indian, you're the Indian!" and laugh and laugh like it was the absolute worst thing in the world to be. I would get so upset. I cried and knew it was true, but was so confused about why it was such a bad thing. As I grew into an adult I secretly longed for connections and historical information about our family. But it wasn't until I reached my early thirties that I finally started to discover myself and to connect with beautiful native people through my career who offered to show me the way.

My grandma would sometimes refer to herself as the last of the Mohicans, even though she was Cree. She just meant that she was the last of the Indians in her family. She was a Cree woman with no status, remaining family members, or any connection to her own history. Because she was a self-proclaimed last Mohican, I knew that she was my only chance to get any information or connection to the heritage I craved.

On the inside, I always knew that I was an Indian, but my family was so confused about what that meant. Their mixed emotions confused me too. We grew up pretty white, I guess, but as I grew into a woman this deep calling kept coming to me. What did it all mean? At the time my grandma was dying, I still had not yet learned to sit with the ancestors by attending a local sweat lodge. I had no connection to my family history.

When I was growing up, my grandparents were alcoholics. Drunken people were everywhere, sipping cheap five-dollar wine all day long. I could often see empty beer bottles around the house.

One beautiful summer day when I was just six years old I was dropped off at my grandparents' house, like I often was. I strutted around in my first brand-new outfit, feeling fine. My light-blue short shorts had a fancy easy slide belt and I had a white t-shirt with stripes and sparkles on it. This brand-new outfit made me so happy; I never got new clothes growing up, so this was a special day indeed. As a middle child, the reality back then was that I got nothing but hand-me-down clothes that were handed down more than once in our very large family. By the time I got the clothes, they were tattered, stained or right out of style.

I had heard that my father was coming to town for a visit. I hardly ever got to see him and I knew I was looking sharp. For a rare moment in my life, I felt beautiful with my brand-new clothes. I even had my picture taken out in the front yard wearing my new outfit because it was such a big deal.

While waiting for the dad that I rarely ever got to see, I patiently sorted buttons from my grandma's old button tin. She had one of those really old Quality Street tins, purple with the fancy lady in her poofy dress and a soldier looking all charming and handsome. She must have had that tin forever. I would spend endless hours sorting her buttons every time I went there because Grandma had absolutely no toys to play with.

One of my favourite drunken friends who always visited at Grandma's house was a tall old thin white man named Roy Sockguy. Well, that wasn't really his last name, but that's how I could pronounce it. He was always so pleasant. A lot of the people who hung around the house were typically drunks and some were definitely creepy, but this guy was different. On this day, like every other time he saw me, he said, "You are something special."

When he said these words, he would look me in the eyes and it felt like he really meant what he said. I remember thinking it was weird because I never really knew him but something felt good about it for sure and I always felt safe with him. It was like he could see inside of me. Most times as a young child I felt like nobody understood me at all except for my grandma. His words stuck with me throughout my entire life. I still reflect back to him and his words when I am down, lost and alone. They bring me much peace and remind me to keep being me.

But despite my excitement over my new clothes and Roy's kind words, my mood was starting to shift. Waiting ever so impatiently for my dad to arrive, I began to pull at my grandma. "How much longer? I am bored!"

To kill some time my loving grandparents gave my four-year-old brother and me a few cents to go to the store and buy ourselves a little something. We had to cross a busy road, four lanes wide, on Main Street to get to the store and would have to cross it again to get back, but we did it. As the hours went by, I began to feel disappointed. No dad, no toys and nobody to show my new clothes to.

So Grandma and Grandpa sent my brother and me to the store one more time to buy them a pack of cigarettes. I remember not wanting to go at all, but felt bad as they had already given us money to buy candy. I felt obligated to do this favour for them.

We headed off to the store and I asked the lady at the counter for a pack of cigarettes. She asked me who were they were for, so I told her and she handed them over to me. As I prepared to cross the road with my little brother once again, I looked back at the big sign over the gas station on Main Street and saw that it read, "$2.25 for cigarettes." Then I heard my wild little brother yell, "GO!" and I saw him take off and make it almost all the way across the street. I hesitated for a second, feeling cautious. But after a couple of seconds, it looked clear so I decided to bolt across the road.

Chapter 2

be.come

That's when a man running a red light on a motorbike struck me down. He had just left the local Legion Pub one block down. Both the motorcycle and I flew high into the air before we landed on the pavement in the middle of the busy street: me first, then he and his bike right on top of me. To this day, I can't recall seeing the man who ran me over. This is just how the story has been told to me by the heroic stranger walking by who pulled us both off the road so neither one of us would get run over by oncoming traffic.

After partially waking up in an ambulance on Main Street, I could hear my parents screaming and yelling at each other about just whose fault this was. The ambulance attendee told them to quiet down. I passed out one more time before waking up some time later on the children's ward of our local hospital. I was lying in bed and feeling very alone. I spent the entire summer in the hospital with pins, screws, and my leg dangling in bed by traction.

That was the summer my grandparents made the choice to do away with the bottles and smokes for good.

Chapter 2

Grandma and Grandpa decided to move to another old low-budget home across from that busy street. They dumped all of their friends and went cold turkey. They dried up and quit smoking. After three months in bed and relearning how to walk, I was thankful to hear that my family was making serious changes. It seemed like Grandma had now turned white, just like her Polish husband, my grandfather.

After that summer, Grandma would not share anything Indian with us. Long gone were the days I would hear her and her drinking buddies speaking the Cree language. Grandma had the typical hard native life. Her family was brutally poor. Her parents were alcoholics. She suffered rape and abuse by a couple of her own family members. She suffered miscarriages, survived on welfare, and lost three of her own children by the time I was born. Surprisingly, through it all, my grandparents remained married for 56 years.

Chapter 2
be.come

In that hospital room in 2010, with her fists up in the air showing me how to make bannock, I know we are close to losing Grandma. I had heard stories about how the dying try to take care of unfinished business before they go. And this was unfinished business for certain.

After years of begging and nagging, the only thing I ever got Grandma to teach me was seven Cree words just a few years prior to her stroke. Two of them were swear words! So this is *it*. I am getting an actual bannock recipe from the real deal, my Indian Grandma. This will officially take me one step closer to being a real Indian and that's all I want. I feel so honoured that she would want this for me and that she is willing to share it with us. Better late than never.

Her hands start digging into the air. Her fists clench tightly. "Oh, Dad," I whisper, "she's kneading the dough."

"What?" He shakes his head as if to say, *This is just crazy.*

"Yes, yes, that's it." We are learning how to make bannock! I am happy and smiling because I know what she wants to do for me, but sad to know that it is almost over with her. I know that soon, I will never be able to see, touch or talk to her ever again.

After what seems like hours, her hands still working hard, I say, "Hey, Grandma, this bannock is fantastic." She continues with the kneading, as if she hasn't heard me. "Grandma, the bannock is delicious. Thank you for teaching me how to make bannock." Gradually, it's as if her face is disappearing. Her eyes never open. But she will not stop kneading the dough with great force.

I feel terrible for her. *This must be exhausting*, I think. My attempts to get her to stop just aren't working. I reach out to my dad and say, "Hey, Dad, isn't this bannock delicious? Mmm?" He does not reply. "Dad!" I say much louder. "Don't you just love this bannock that Grandma taught us how to make?" Finally, in a very resistant tone, he says, "Uh, yeah, sure."

Hearing my dad's words of approval is all Grandma needs to surrender her hands. With great appreciation for the lesson, I hold her hands and help her bring them back down to her almost lifeless body. I listen to her very wet shallow breathing. It is late, almost midnight, and the only ones left in the room are my dad, my oldest cousin, myself and, of course, Grandma. The three of us are her cheer squad, her support system, and always there for her.

Grandma is getting very tired. When she finally opens her eyes and looks at me, my heart is breaking. She beckons me toward her. I walk up, take her hands, and look into her small grey eyes. "Yes, Grandma?" She looks back at me and says, "It's time for you to go now," and points towards the door.

My chest is filling up with stress, my nerves are trembling, but still I have no tears. I look around the room and notice that my dad and cousin are still there, apparently allowed to stay. I don't ask any questions; I know what's going to happen. I reach over to her, grab her hands, put my face almost nose to nose with her and whisper, "Grandma, don't forget about the pictures."

After a long pause, she looks at me directly in the eye and asks, "Do you mean that?"

Chapter 2

"Yes," I confidently confirm. One final glance and away I go.

Even though my grandma and I loved each other to bits, we never once say it to each other. Perhaps we don't need to.

After a ten-minute drive up the hill, I am home. I tuck myself into bed. About an hour later, I get the call to come back to the hospital. Grandma is gone. I race back down to be with my dad and cousin. The room is empty, without a trace of Grandma. Who would I go to now when I needed someone? What would I do without her? I was at a complete loss. I was just empty.

My dad, cousin and I head over to her house to tell Grandpa. We had sent him home to rest as we knew it was going to be a sleepless night for all. Grandpa is not surprised by our news. He handles the news well.

Her house feels empty; her presence is still there but I can feel that her body is gone. It is a strong feeling. It already

Chapter 2

be.come

feels very different for me. Nobody can believe that she is no longer going to be around. We are all devastated, sad and unsure of what this means for Grandpa. I know I am feeling something really unique; I feel like I can feel her soul and that it is now up, up somewhere above me. I can feel her but I can't see her. All I know is that I promised her I would look for her and wait for any sign that she might send. I am ready when she is.

the experiment begins

chapter 3

Grandma keeps her promise…

Chapter 3

be.come

On a Saturday night in August, six months after Grandma's passing, I am in bed sleeping deeply. At approximately 4:00 AM in the morning I awake to a large **BANG**. My husband, a firefighter who sleeps really lightly for his job, never hears a thing. He is sound asleep.

I sit up and shout, "Oh my God, what was that?"

My husband dozily asks, "What was what?"

"That noise, that really loud noise! It sounded like a bookshelf falling over."

"It's just one of your dreams… go back to bed… there was no sound."

My position in the bed allows me to see down the hall where the children sleep. I peer intently down the dark hall. I listen carefully and finally agree that nothing has fallen. I go back to sleep for the night.

In the morning, I rise from bed, still replaying the loud noise in my head and the strange feeling that came with it. My normal routine is to walk down the hall, see if the kids are awake and wish them a good morning. So first I walk past my teenage daughter's room and see that she is still sleeping. I keep going and turn into my six-year-old son's room.

As I enter his room, I step on something that really hurts. I bend down to find a large photo in a frame. It is my grandma. It's a portrait I took of her a few years back, looking beautiful and glowing. She wore her fancy white blouse, lipstick, and pearl earrings. It was the photo we had printed for her funeral. I am stunned. *What the*

Chapter 3

be.come

heck was this doing on my son's floor? There is not a mark, not a scratch on it, and the nail is still stuck tightly in the wall in the hallway where it usually hangs.

I yell for my husband to come and see this.

"What's up?" he says, still not concerned.

I point to the photo of Grandma on the floor and say in a baffled mumble, "How did that happen?"

"Well... the house must have shifted. It is an old house and that sort of thing happens."

"It can't be. It fell off the wall, rolled five or six feet down the hall, then turned a corner and went into our son's room and the nail is still in the wall! It must be Grandma! That loud bang in the middle of the night, now this!"

I ask my son and daughter if they heard anything — a loud bang, the picture falling, anything? They both say they didn't. I am flabbergasted. *How can this be possible?* I think about it all day but my husband keeps insisting nothing strange has happened.

The following Sunday night at approximately 9:30 PM, I am working away in my home office on a submission for a business award. My banker had insisted I complete it before the deadline the next morning at 9:00 AM. I typically would never leave an important task like this until the last minute but I know this award is way out of my league. I mean, my banker of all people should know that I am not in the running for a national award like this. But he told me I was picking up momentum and that they hold it for two years. He maintains that if I keep going the way I am, things could turn out great for me.

After putting it off and hoping I could cut and paste all the important information into the application, I planned to get through it as painlessly as possible. Submitting for business awards generally requires a lot of work and a lot of desire, and I was lacking the desire part.

Chapter 3

I pull out my laptop and dig around for my most current business plan before emailing it over to my desktop computer. I hear a *bling* sound and see that I have a new email pop-up that reads "To Tryna, from Tryna, subject: business plan." Then seconds later I hear another *bling* and see another email notification — strangely I have received another email from myself. *Strange*, I thought. The second email has no subject line. I open it and almost fall out of my chair.

This time there was no denying what was happening.

The email is dated March 20, 2010. My grandma died March 27, 2010, and it is now August 29, 2010. I yell for my husband and he comes swiftly down the hall.

"What is it?"

I point to the screen and say, "Look!"

"It's a picture of your grandma and cousin. So?" He smirked.

Chapter 3

"I have never seen that photo before in my life! I never took it. And look who sent it to me."

He inspects the email. "It says it's from you?"

"Uh-huh. And look at the date it says today is!"

"March 20."

"Yup. What date is it?"

He laughed, "August 29. My birthday."

"So how can that be?" I ask.

My husband has no interest in computers and avoids them at all costs. He has no idea why or how this could have happened. I say, with no small amount of sarcasm, "Maybe it happened because the house shifted."

I contact my cousin, who also has limited computer skills, and ask her if she emailed the photo to me. She confirms

be.come

that she never did and that she doesn't even know how to email a photo.

The next morning I call my dad as soon as I can. "Dad, you are never going to believe what's happened! Your mother is here!"

Few things excite my dad. He has two modes: calm, chill, and unattached, or raging mad. I rarely witness much in the middle in the way of other emotions from him. So he calmly replies, "Oh? Well, what are you so worked up about? You are the one that asked her to come."

"What? Dad!" Strangely, my body starts to feel freezing cold. I jump on the couch and wrap myself in a bunch of blankets to finish speaking with my dad. "This is just crazy. Why am I so cold?" I am never cold; I am usually complaining of being too hot.

"Well, it sounds like you got what you wanted. You asked for her to come and she did."

"No, no, no," I shriek. "This is freaky and creepy. I feel weird." My dad just laughs. For some reason, he's not surprised by what's happening.

A good while after Grandma's death, I have this dream of my son and I standing in my teenage daughter's dorm room in another city. Although my daughter isn't in the room, I know we are at her place and I can feel her. It is late into the evening and my nine-year-old son and I are outside standing on the deck, looking at the moonlight.

For some reason, I turn around to see my grandma walking in the door wearing rich fancy clothes, a beautiful set of pearls wrapped around her neck. She sparkles with diamonds like a rich person. She is smiling, and her teeth are perfectly straight and white and absolutely gorgeous. Her walk is smooth and elegant, and she holds a classy little purse. She looks like a million dollars and isn't afraid to show off her new image and energy to me.

Chapter 3

be.come

When she was alive, she would wear her nicest pressed slacks and blouse from the Salvation Army, but her teeth were not straight and she was missing a few — it made her native accent much stronger. But in the dream it was as though she had become royalty or famous.

I am so happy to see her! I say, "Grandma, you're here?" She hugs my son and I tightly. We are all so happy and we just can't quit hugging. I ask, "How are you here? Why are you here?" She won't respond with words. After a few short moments, she starts to walk away.

"Grandma! Wait, don't go, please," I beg. Standing in the doorframe with her back to me, she turns her head around and says with a huge smile on her face, "I know what kind of jam you like." She walks out of the door and out of my dream.

After waking up, I feel disappointed that she's gone but thankful for the experience. I try to make sense of it logically, but decide that I just cannot. About a month after that, I tell my dad the story.

He pauses for a moment and says, "Oh, guess what?"

"What?" I ask.

He tells me a story about an incident that happened at his office. My dad is a superintendent for a large industrial welding company in the same city where my daughter went to college. He says, in a slightly hesitant and surprised voice, that a box of empty jam jars and labels just like Grandma used to use were sitting on his desk at work one morning when he arrived. He asked everybody in the office where they came from. Nobody seemed to know anything. He took the jars home.

Now he knows who gave them to him.

Yes, Grandma was keeping her end of the bargain. The experiment was progressing. But little did I know how far she would take it.

breaking down to build back up

chapter 4

the healing begins and the
seed for this book is sown…

M y first encounter with Ruby is at my photography studio when she comes in looking for a donation, not too long after Grandma's death. Financially speaking, I am tapped out at the time. Business is slow and I am emotionally out of gas. I am in no mood for silliness — it is only springtime and I am already done giving donations out for the year.

Plus, Grandma is visiting me quite a bit. I don't understand it. It scares me. I'm not doing well at all.

I tell Ruby that I can't help her with a donation for her event and start to walk away.

Chapter 4

"My event," she explains confidently, "is a psychic fair and I thought you would be a good fit."

"A good fit? Why on earth would I be a good fit for the psychic fair?" I ignorantly ask, shaking my head.

Ruby is approximately five feet, two inches tall, with a full figure and the most beautiful blue eyes. Large soft waves run through her medium-brown shoulder-length hair. Her personality seems gentle and trustworthy. She seems to have the loving energy of an auntie.

Our eyes dance around, scoping each other out. Yes, there is something different about her, so I ask her what exactly she does at a psychic fair anyway.

"I am a Spirit Writer," she says.

"A what?"

"Well," she hesitantly initiates, "it appears that I am writing you a letter…" and then after a long pause to confirm that I am listening, she continues, "but actually it's your guides,

Chapter 4

be.come

your angels, so to speak, communicating with me, and I just pass their message on to you."

Pfft! What? Guides? Angels? Oh my God, what is she talking about?

My facial expressions and body language are so intense and rude they probably could break glass. Does she think I'm stupid? I can't believe what I am hearing. Just when you think you're already at the bottom, some strange lady comes and tries to tell you she's a Spirit Writer and wants you to help her.

Ruby hands me her business card and a magazine that contains her ad and says, "If you change your mind, this is how you can find me." She saunters out the front door, not looking back. Without any hesitation I immediately throw her card and magazine into the recycling bin. There is no way I am ever going to pay $150 an hour for some lady to scribble on a piece of paper and tell me that the spirits want to talk to me.

Chapter 4

But after trying to deal with all of these visits from my dead Grandma, noticing my body temperatures change from hot to cold with her presence, and many other personal and professional ordeals, I know I need help.

I'm having dreams that fill me with wonder and confusion. In one of them, I am on a beautiful island, which is very lush and green. My son and I are on a playground with monkey bars, slides and big wooden structures. I watch him play, feeling joyful.

Suddenly, an enormous white bear floats through the air towards us, paddling his legs like a trotting horse. He is gliding so quickly I have no time to protect myself or my son. He comes to a rest suspended in the air in front of me, with his face inches from mine. He is purring like a cat. Our noses touch and I reach out to touch the bear's soft white fur. It feels as if my hands are falling in love with the bear, receiving a powerful vibration from the core of this magical animal. His being says to me: "LOVE."

Once I understand the bear's message, he looks me in the eye and showers me with the most divine feeling I have ever experienced. He bows his head as if to thank me for receiving his gift and floats away.

I find out that the white bear is likely my spirit animal, giving me a special message to change the course of my life. Is my native blood stirring? Are my ancestors trying to get in touch with me? What does all of this mean?

I decide to hire a well-known local traditional therapist to bail me out of this dark place. However, once I get to her office, she simply tells me that I am fine and don't need her help. She feels sure I can get through the situation on my own! This is a defining moment in my life; who goes to a counselor and isn't taken in? How would she know in just a few minutes that I was fine?

I *am* at my bottom. The problem is that I don't look like I have anything wrong with me. I have a good professional reputation and a wonderful husband and children who are all successful in their own right. My life probably looks picture-perfect to the therapist, but on the inside — the part nobody can see with their eyes — I am honestly broken.

My friend Tina starts telling me about something called the chakra system. There are seven main chakras, she explains, and they are located along the spine, extending out of the front and back of the body. Each chakra represents our highest level of vibration and spiritual awareness. Every one of them has a different field of brilliance that corresponds to aspects of our daily life and current physical energy. They spin like wheels and can be manipulated in both positive and negative ways to shift the energy you feel in different parts of your body and life. My friend says that understanding this will help me change some of my energy and the emotions that are going on inside of me.

I go online, take a free course on balancing the chakras, and start to sob instantly after doing the first exercise. Tears are streaming down my face for the first time that I can remember since I was a little girl. I am a real mess, but nobody in my world knows just how bad it is except a couple of very close girlfriends. Not even my husband or children know how lost I feel.

The trouble I have is that I am generally strong and people don't recognize when I am at my bottom because I hold myself together very well most of the time. When I don't, my emotions typically turn into anger, not tears. In the end, people don't realize that I am struggling and I end up dealing with my emotions alone.

At the drop of the first tear during this chakra-rebalancing exercise, I know I need help. My first attempt to reach out for help with the therapist had gone disappointingly sideways, but I instantly remember my strange encounter with Ruby.

I jump into my vehicle, head down to my office and desperately search for her business card. Since one week has already passed, it is difficult to find it through all of the other papers in the bin. Panic starts to set in. Ruby is the only resource I feel I can try at this time. I am desperate for some help and this is now my only option, logical or not. Lost in my mind and heart, I sit on the floor and search for almost an hour until I finally recover the card amongst all the other stuff in the bag. I hold it in my hands, pull it towards my heart and pray that this will somehow help me. Would there be a light at the end of this long dark tunnel?

Pulling up to her house I am so nervous that I park a long way down the road so people won't see my vehicle in her driveway. I am embarrassed that I have hit an all-time low and am now getting counseling from supposed dead people and angels!

Ruby greets me at her front door. As I enter her home, tears start to fall. I let them. Her office is pleasant, with relaxing spa-type music playing. Her desk is neat, tidy and professionally decorated. Upon sitting down, I start to ask a lot of questions. "What do we do? Should I talk? Do I listen? How does this go anyway?" I shift around frantically in my seat.

"You are coming from ego," Ruby says gently, "and you will now learn how to come from essence."

I have no idea what she is talking about and it sounds really weird so I pull back in my chair. I hold my words back, tighten my neck and put my chest up in fight mode. *Ego? How dare she say ego! I don't have an ego! Seriously, who is this lady, anyway,* I think to myself.

"See, you just did it again," says Ruby. "You literally pulled yourself back, your energy felt dense, and you emotionally closed down on me. Ego doesn't always mean showing off or bragging. What I am talking about is the exterior place you are coming from. How you use your energy to protect yourself when you react to things in life. Essence is using that innate energy inside of you," she continues softly. "Essence is the opposite of ego. But don't worry; we actually need both in our lives."

I sit and try hard to make some sense of what she is saying, but I can't. It is way over my head. But for some reason, I stay, watching her pen scribble on the paper extremely fast and listen to the rest of what she has to say.

Her final words of that particular session end with: "There will be a book that you are going to write. Two years, pen to paper."

I laugh out loud. "No, that will not be happening. I hate reading books and I am terrible with grammar." In my mind, that's all I need to prove to myself that the appointment with her is just a waste of time and money.

But the session is a slap in the face. Afterward, I feel forced to look within. *Could this be true? Could that hard-edged egotistical person she's referring to really be me?*

By the time of this appointment with Ruby, Grandma has already been gone approximately one year. Her visits through my sleeping dreams are frequent. I am really scared of the times when I can feel her around me when I am awake. I cannot ignore what is going on any longer.

I am actually going to have to start looking inside myself to see what is really going on. I got the tidbit of information I apparently need from Ruby, but I have no idea how all of this transformation and learning about essence and ego will actually happen. It is all so foreign to me.

Ruby also mentioned to me during the session that I have two spirits with me: one is my mother's mother's mother and the other is my grandma, my dad's mother. *Could this be real?* I wonder. *Am I some kind of sucker for punishment that I would even consider believing all of this nonsense?*

Growing up, I knew that I was worth so much more than what I was given, emotionally and materialistically. But when I looked in the mirror and saw this scrawny, tall, boyish native girl with short hair, I would look up and ask someone in the sky why life had to be so hard. I felt like nobody could see who I really was: a kind, loving, big-hearted girl who always wanted to please. But nobody else saw it. Nobody ever came to my rescue.

Chapter 4

Over the years, through my teens to my mid-thirties, I had emotionally shut down from all the crap I endured growing up. I successfully stripped almost all of my own emotions away so that life could be easier. Being sensitive and feeling everything as a child made for hard times. As an adult, my friendships didn't last because I would expect too much from people and didn't understand why they didn't want better for themselves. I couldn't stand to visit with gossips and backstabbers. I would be frustrated by their inability to problem-solve or create positive changes in their own lives. I mean, isn't that what life is about? Making change, becoming better than we were yesterday? This was my core belief. I constantly focused on achieving more than I had and always strove to be a better person than I was yesterday. For the life of me, I could not understand why some people were okay with just being mediocre.

But I had been busy building a thick brick wall around my own heart. I had been distracting myself by proving myself externally — winning awards, meeting celebrities. And I had no idea just how emotionally hard I had become. I had no tolerance for anyone's shortcomings and always believed that I deserved to be treated well by others. If I wasn't treated well, I took out my most reliable self-defense tool to solve the problems that could come up. They were my invisible scissors. I used them to cut that cord that connected us immediately, and out of my life they went. I was judgmental and said things like, "What's wrong with people? Why are they making stupid choices? Are they blind, gutless or just oblivious?"

Sedona
part 1
chapter 5

love…

Chapter 5

be.come

When I arrive at the writers' retreat in Sedona, Arizona in March 2016, I find a small space at the edge of a small table at the back of the room. I am in a packed house of potential authors who are all waiting to write the next big one.

My own ego is tucked away ever so neatly because I don't need it anymore. I actually know what an ego is, why we have one, and when to use it. This time I have left it at home. I really just want to get the book I began last year finished so that I can move on to the next phase of my journey.

Chapter 5

The first phase of the book occurred in Grande Prairie, Alberta, with the same writing teacher who is facilitating this retreat in Sedona. At the time, I could hardly believe what I was doing: the prophecy Ruby had spoken to me about the book appeared to be coming true. I felt compelled to attend the retreat in Grande Prairie — there was just no fighting it. Then, while I was there, Grandma communicated to me in fantastical visions, in pictures that had tremendous emotional meaning but little verbal or logical sense.

I simply recorded them, feeling carried along on Grandma's powerful current. That current kept carrying me until I found myself in Sedona.

I really don't know why I felt the driving urge to write a book in the first place, but I did. It isn't something I ever imagined I would be doing at this stage of my life. I wish I could work alone for stuff like this, I really do. I have all of my writing gear piled up on the table in front of me. I feel a bit claustrophobic and I would love to have more space to make sure I can connect with my higher self.

Chapter 5

be.come

The truth is, I'm hoping Grandma will show up to help me complete everything by the end of the week. In order to connect and channel her in, I really need to be free and able to have lots of physical space around me.

I have a feeling that big things are going to happen from this experience. Luckily I have already made some instant career connections and a new friend. I even got a free room upgrade at my hotel to a two-bedroom spa-themed penthouse that would have normally cost $900 a night! *How did that happen?* I keep sending gratitude out to my guides and Grandma. I registered for the retreat just seven days before it started, so all the rooms should have been booked up.

Everything in my last-minute planning had already turned out far better than I could have ever expected. I am excited and anxiously awaiting what's in store for me at the retreat. *Certainly it's going to blow my mind*, I thought, *because whenever I get this special feeling, it always does.* It's always so unpredictable (in a good way) when you allow your guides to step in and present opportunities to you. Many times incredible things show up for you, but you have to be willing to notice and follow them.

Chapter 5

Now knowing how to use my intuition almost on demand, I sit up in my chair with perfect posture and imagine opening my third chakra up like a big steel industrial wheel. The third chakra is the space above the belly button and below the ribs. This is the place I physically use to receive messages from Spirit. It's the place where most people say they feel a *gut instinct*. It is a major psychic receptive area.

To open it, I intentionally visualize cranking that wheel to the right. I imagine the energy flow from high above coming down to me in the stomach area. Sometimes this feels like an umbilical cord that runs from my chakra to the sky. Once I do that, I take a few very deep breaths, let them out, and follow through with an *ahhh* sound. After releasing stress, weight or heavy thoughts, this always puts me instantly into a meditative state where I can receive direct messages from guides, and more specifically, my grandma.

Meditation is the tool I always use to access my higher knowing and to do any psychic medium work. It allows me to channel or bring in different people who have died so I can talk with them. It takes me to that next level of connection.

The afterlife's characters are just like they were when they were alive. I pick up on their personalities first, and then start to see their physical body in my imagination or with my third eye. Typically, in the early stages of meditating, most people are just trying to achieve a state of peace by clearing their mind and allowing new fresh ideas and thoughts to come in. But I naturally have an ability that takes me to a special place when I do it. Thankfully, most times I can turn it off and on at my own discretion.

Looking around the room at the writers' retreat, I feel like a fish in a fish bowl. I feel that nothing I have would make me or my book stand out from anyone else's in the room. Nevertheless, I feel prepared and somewhat in the zone. I just know somehow that it will all work out.

In my imagination, I respectfully request for Grandma to come in and join me so that we can get started with the day's work. And sure enough, she comes — but not too strongly. I can feel her energy here, but she isn't really coming forward. This is so unusual. *Why is she doing this? I wonder. This really isn't like her. She has never done this to me before.*

Then, to my complete surprise, the first being that comes forward with a message isn't a human being at all. It's my dog! Hershey, my 12-year-old chocolate lab who passed away just over a year ago, is coming through to me. *Weird!* I am shocked. I have never connected with a dead animal before. She was always one of those dogs who protected her family completely, but had a bit of arrogance and liked to be alone.

After a few moments of shock realizing that Hershey is with me, I fixate on what she might have to say. *That is such a gift. A dog came through? My beloved dog!* I can't be more overjoyed to feel her presence again.

Hershey tells me I have learned what I needed to know; that I have learned to have confidence as I write this book. She lovingly tells me that I am also loyal, loving, proud and direct — just like her. She wants to let me know that she is actually here guiding and walking with me, hoping that

Chapter 5
be.come

I will find my own way towards publishing this book. She says that she is proud of me, and that she's still at the house where she always sat outside, overlooking the beautiful view of the valley. She says she is talking to me from that special spot in my yard. She softly says that she is home and not to worry about her as she is happy all of the time. She knows that I hurt inside sometimes but that I am not really alone. She tells me that she is always with me.

"You look just like me," she whispers, "fast, brown, smart, physical, and even our bodies were built the same way!" She laughs. "You are all of these things: the watcher, the looker and the protector. You can do it!" she cheers. "This is it. You are really ready to write this book!"

"I love you, Hershey. I am so pleased it's you," I say, speaking the words only in my mind. I thank her for coming. Then, when I send her my love, her energy vanishes away. Suddenly, I can feel Grandma stepping forward. *Ahh, what a relief.*

"Grandma," I say with my inner voice, "I know that you are here because I can feel you, and I am ready!"

She is there but sitting back a bit. "So, Grandma," I say, hopeful that she will carry me along, "what do you want me to start with?"

Her response is quick and blunt: "Start with whatever you want."

I feel nervous. I tell her I don't want to make a mistake.

"There will be no mistakes," she says. "It just is. It's time to tell the people what we know and it's happy and easy. Just tell it like it is. Tell them the real story. It's not about you, it's about becoming."

She feels so present but won't lead me in the writing this time. *Darn.* I really want her to lead so I won't have to be responsible for the outcome of this book. I feel lost about writing and don't have a clue as to how to write an actual book. But I guess that's the point. Grandma says it's time to do it. I have to figure it out and ask for help when I need it; that's one of my lessons. I am not great at asking anyone for help but will clearly need it to finish this assignment.

Chapter 5

be.come

She told me once before to start in the middle. That logically didn't make any sense to me. *Shouldn't I start at the beginning?* I wondered. So I repeat: "Where do I start this story, Grandma?"

"Start it in the middle," she stresses.

"Middle? What? Why the middle?"

For a few moments, she simply tells me that it will be a good book and that I will be rewarded for my efforts in some way or another. She tells me to just trust in the process.

As I sit in my chair with my head down, meditating, I visualize Grandma putting the book in my hands and then see it opening itself up to the middle of the book. I am very used to listening to the guidance I hear from her now, so I would never ignore these directions. *Middle it is,* I confirm to myself.

"This page is about love, love, love," says Grandma. "The highlight of the book always goes back to love." She laughs.

"I already know that, though," I happily answer.

When I had the first dream about this book in 2013, I learned that it was about love. I had a sleeping dream that a book was coming into my life. I didn't necessarily know why I was going to write one, but my dream showed me a worm turning into a butterfly. Upon awakening, I knew that it signified metamorphosis.

In that same dream I was gifted with the title: *be.come.* I could see the word spelled out. The dream was so specific that I even saw where the title was placed on the book cover and what font the guides wanted me to use. This is when I knew that they were telling me to do something; the ideas just simply came to me.

The year before this visit to Sedona, when I wrote the initial draft of the book in Grande Prairie, I wrote it like a how-to manual. It was almost completely about how to make self-improvements to become a better person so that love finds you more often. When I sat down before going to Sedona and re-read it, I realized that Grandma had actually written the book through me. She wrote it specifically for me, so that I could learn how to be.come and then share my lessons with everyone else.

The fact is, I had spent the last year literally acting out all of the instructions she wrote in that book myself. But since I never read it again after I wrote it, I had no idea that it was for me until I was getting ready for Arizona.

"You were preparing me, weren't you, Grandma?" Seated at my small space at the writers' table, I have an *a-ha* moment. The concept of love climaxes in the middle of the book — that's what she wanted me to realize.

I sink into a deep meditative state and Grandma delivers a profound message: "Love others unlike yourself so that you can learn how to truly love yourself. As you start this practice, people will start coming to you that you will not expect or understand in the beginning. It's easier to love others more than yourself right now. But when it's returned to you, you will learn unconditional love. Isn't that easy?

"Do not focus on self-love right now, only focus on giving it out. When you wholeheartedly give it out it will absolutely come back to you — don't try to understand. It's simply the law of attraction: what you put out always comes back to you. Give good, receive good; give bad, shallow thoughts, or lies, then you will receive them all back. It will take the pressure off you when you focus on giving rather than receiving. Then you will know where you are at, and what your ability to output love is, by observing what's coming into you. That's it for now."

Wow. I shake my body around, come back to reality, and know that Grandma's message has to be written down immediately, so I do that. In my logical mind I am baffled. For the life of me, I cannot believe her wise words. That was not the Grandma I grew up with. As loving and kind as she was in real life, there is no way she would have ever spoken like that to anyone. But it is her. She is now somehow different, yet the same.

Suddenly, I hear the voice of one my guides: "As you are continuing the journey, the rest will come from Grandma."

For a moment, I sit wondering if people at this retreat would judge me if I told them about having guides. *Of course they would.* People have so many hangups about so many different things.

"Ultimately they're burdened by their own judgments," Grandma interjects. "They are especially burdened about too much giving and not enough receiving in their own worlds. Really — it's true. People always wonder what's in it for them first. They want it given to them first before they are willing to give it out." Grandma casually directs my attention back to the law of attraction, saying, "Most people do it backwards. If you really want something, you have to give it out so that you can create the energy or situation of having it come to you."

"We should focus on self-love then?" I ponder. I'm not sure I'm really understanding her.

"No, the pressure is too high," she states wisely. "People everywhere are hurting deep inside and they need to practice giving it first. Then they will have no choice but to receive it down the road. It's inevitable."

Chapter 5

I'm confused. I'm hoping Grandma knows what she is talking about. I really feel like her energy has changed a lot since last year when I started to write this book. She feels so much more worldly, like a master teacher of sorts. I can feel how serious she is about teaching. I also notice that she's much more of an observer now and is letting me do whatever I want throughout the writing process.

Still, I constantly look to her and continually ask for her guidance. She is almost always there for me in spirit. Sometimes I feel like she doesn't exactly come to my rescue, as she's not helping me do my writing work as much as I want. She seems to prefer that I make my own decisions now. I could always count on her to show me that love will help solve all of my problems and she is here now to hold space for me when I call out to her.

But I have no idea why I would be asked to write a book. I don't like reading or writing, I can't spell, and I am terrible with grammar. My audiobook library is large, but I think I have only read two or three actual books in my entire adult life! I think about all the professionals on every level whom I will need to recruit to even get this thing to print.

There must be some mistake, I think. "You have the wrong person for this assignment!" I say to any guide who might be listening. But Grandma points to the paper and directs me to focus on writing.

"Okay, so we've learned that love comes in many forms, and that what we actually see is a reflection of what we put out?" I confirm with Grandma.

"Simple and common sense, you might think," she replies. "But is it? Do we as a human nation really practice this? I believe it's not often enough."

"So love solves all problems," I exclaim. "I would like to tell you that I have experienced a number of situations, experiences and conversations with people whom I know and love who do not feel that love will solve all of their problems. I have literally gone head to head and lost long-term friendships over this exact conversation."

Chapter 5

"Not all, but many," she chides. "If we used this free, easy ace of hearts to move forward in the game of life, what could that look like? How many small changes would happen? Collectively all the smalls would grow into large. But it starts really small at first and I mean *ever* so small. If it's done right, nobody will even realize that the great shift is happening. One day all common people will see and feel a shift in the universal consciousness of the world and war will no longer be the major subject of human problems."

I can really feel her around me now. It's so strong. It's like she went and got a masterful education once she crossed over to the other side. When she was alive, she often spoke of her lack of education and how she never made it past grade 2 or 3. She taught herself how to read and write over the years, but was never taken to school after the first couple of grades. She always spoke about how she wished things had been different.

"Is that even possible?" I hesitantly inquire. "I mean, really, who would ever believe that's possible with all that's going on in the world? We may be seeing World War III in the making with so many political and religious wars, terrorists, global warming and cancer. Fear is plaguing the whole world."

"This is how it has to happen," she insists. "It really has to start small, so small that it's easy and manageable for all peoples. I mean so simple that even this entire book must be written in a very basic language so as not to cause confusion about the topic. So many times people think that life is hard and crippling, so they just do nothing, and don't try to make change or express their feelings or ideas the way they really want to. Many people feel that by doing nothing they can avoid any judgment about the role they play in life.

"Kindness and love are the only answers to life's challenges. If you practice using love and kindness to solve problems and integrate them into your current resolution strategies, all the dynamics of any given situation will completely change. Every single situation is changeable if you want it to be changed. Changing something sometimes requires you to really go deep within yourself and ask if you even want to shift the way you usually handle problems. By that I mean solving them with your heart. Do you really want it to change, Birdie? Many people don't like change; they fear it."

"Grandma, I have already learned that you can't change people. I have actually tried and failed miserably over and over."

"You got it wrong the first time," she retorts bluntly. "What you need to do is change yourself first and how you look at love. But don't be too hard on yourself. You have already come such a long way. You are doing it correctly now for the most part and that's all that matters."

"Love has no real course though," I point out. "The dictionary definition of love is: unselfish, loyal and benevolent concern for the good of another person. Many believe it is only defined as the following: affection and tenderness felt by lovers. There are actually several different dictionary definitions, but who has the right to declare what it really means? There are so many components to love. How can you just tell someone that they should love and leave it at that? And who gets to teach you this concept?"

Chapter 5

be.come

"Actually, Birdie, you are the only one that can teach yourself how to love. It's your journey and process of becoming. Becoming love is the most elementary state of being. We have all un-learned it and have guarded and protected ourselves from it. People protect their hearts in a way that no one on the other side can understand, and that's why I am here." Then, her voice becomes commanding as she says, "It's time to tell the people to go back to the most basic human skill and emotion. This is the absolute secret to world evolution and will break down war."

"It seems ridiculously obvious, but we still don't know how to do it," I say, shaking my head.

"Yes, you do. You all do, you just *think* that you don't and that's the problem. You're all doing way too much thinking and not enough feeling. Get out of your heads and into your hearts. You need to go first. Going first is actually really easy," she murmurs.

"Tell me how?" I sarcastically bark. "I don't want to be responsible for this lesson all on my own. I will write your book, but since you asked me to do this, you have to tell me how it works."

"Okay," she says, indulging me. "Just make sure that you are listening because I am only going to say this once. **OPEN YOUR HEARTS**. It's an action, not a thought."

"Okay," I agree, tentatively. "But just how do we open a heart? Other than open-heart surgery, how the heck would a person actually open a heart?"

Grandma snickers. "Quit trying so hard, Birdie. It's not your job — you're just writing this down. Remember?"

I laugh. "Okay, okay, so now what?"

"The opening of one's heart," she explains, "is an action that needs to be stated or asked for first; that's the first step. Many people don't actually want to open their heart. They are afraid of what they will find out about themselves. They say that they worry about what other people think of them, but that's not true. It's that they fear what they truly think of themselves.

"People *think* that they are worrying about what others think of them so they act a certain way. But really, it's because they are so afraid to truly look at *themselves* and look inside, you know, to who they really are. They distract themselves with what's going on on the outside of them, not looking at and truly loving who is on the inside. It's a complete distraction of self. It *appears* to work for most people, but generally they do remain unhappy for a long time."

"So with that said, wouldn't it make logical sense to start working on loving yourself first?"

"NO!" Grandma is adamant. "It's just too hard for most people. They need to practice loving others first."

"What will happen next, Grandma? Please tell me more. I really need to hear this."

"When people really start being kind to others and actually looking every single person in the eye, real change can start. They will literally change the emotional wiring inside of themselves. Remember what happened to you when you did that, Birdie?"

I immediately recall a time when I was 23 years old or so, and in some kind of deep depression. Nobody, including myself, would have said that I was depressed, but now, looking back, the signs were so clear. I slept all of the time. I had naps everywhere I went. My attitude was brutally negative and I was a continual grump. Everyone around me made me mad.

When I was in this deep hole, I heard a message. I simply knew my life needed to shift for the better. The idea seemed to come to me out of nowhere. I decided to be excessively nice for one whole week. Seven days of pure, over the top, sickening niceness. I was being an angry, bitter, sarcastic jerk when I was fantasizing this plan in my head. You know, *pfft* this and *idiots* that about pretty much everything and everyone. But I did know that deep down I was a miserable mess. So that little voice inside of me clearly told me to shape up. It told me I had to fix myself because I had indeed created my situation.

Chapter 5

be.come

I started off by going to a local grocery store and holding the door open to let everyone else go in first. I fake-smile at them and try to look them in the eyes but many times in the beginning of this experiment I was so angry that I would not be able to look at them at all. I noticed that this person didn't say thank you, or that person was lazy. Some people just ignored me. But I kept the deal with myself no matter what and continued on because I trusted that message that I heard from somewhere out there.

After about three days I noticed that there was a shift. A couple of people here and there started to look me in the eyes briefly and thank me for holding the door. I was starting to see change slowly. I randomly caught myself hoping that the next person would reach out with some kind of responsive kindness.

On about day four or five, it actually happened: an elderly lady said thank you in a way that just felt really good inside. I wanted more of that. My instincts were to be nicer, so I did that, and what I found was that the nicer I got, the nicer almost all the other people got too. It became easier when there was a silent person or a rude non-thanker passing through. Interestingly enough, I felt like I could see more going on within them. I started to feel a bit of compassion for them. Somehow, I felt like I just knew there was more going on with them than met the eye. So for the next few days, I would simply observe them: their behaviours, body language, facial expressions and voice tone.

Thinking about the niceness experiment in Sedona, at Grandma's prompting, I realize how simple it is. So simple that you would have thought it was taught to us in kindergarten. But do we ever actually observe ourselves out and about at a grocery store? Holding doors or letting other people go first? Do we notice if we look people in the eye? Do we think about whether we are being authentic, note our moods, and try to make genuine eye contact with strangers?

I realize that this grocery store experiment was my first lesson in love, seventeen years ago, a lesson taught to me by my higher self. That day in the grocery store I decided I was going to do my best to try to be better in order to shift my life for the next seventeen years. That's the only action I took. It was all I felt I could do in that stage of my life. Who knew it would play such a significant role in my future?

Grandma speaks up again. "Yes, and now look at you. You are sharing what you've learned with so many now. And because of that, people will be able to know that they are not alone and will walk with you on your journey. Going first is hard, and if nobody ever went first at anything, what would the world look like?"

"Grandma, that doesn't even make sense. Everything has to be started by someone and I did not start this!"

"I never actually said you started anything, I just said that you went first. Going first is all about demonstrating what you have come to learn and that it's necessary for somebody to go first."

"Going first and starting something?" I am still confused as to how they are different. "Can you please clarify?"

"Let's take this book, for example," Grandma says. "One: going first means that you have chosen to go forward with what you know: believing, seeing, feeling or trusting when it doesn't appear that anyone is going to understand you or support what you have created. So you need to have the guts to go first. Nothing too serious, just listening and following through with what you know to be true.

"Two: starting something means that you've invented it from absolute nothing to something. Contrary to popular belief, Thomas Edison did not actually invent the light bulb, but he was the first to create the entire electric utility system so he could power his bulbs. Look at what light has done for the entire world.

"Birdie, you did not invent love, you are just being asked to go first and to get a movement happening. If people like what they feel, they will move forward and that's all you need to know."

"Well, okay, but what if I screw it up? What will happen to your fine message?"

"You won't," she whispered, and left it at that.

Chapter 5

be.come

I take a gulp, and pray that she knows what she's talking about. So far I have seen nothing but good things from Grandma, so I trust, let go, and onward I go.

Her word sounds so simple, but why would I be assigned to *love*? When I look around, there is war happening everywhere: the usual Middle Eastern countries, but now Canada, the U.S. and Europe are all being targeted as well. People are really scared and confused. They will likely laugh at this seemingly dim-witted idea right now. They don't have time for practical jokes.

"This is a pivotal moment of history in the making," Grandma steadfastly declares.

My guides are clearly asking for some help from me. *Why me?* I wonder. *What can I even do? I am just one person living in a little northern Canadian city and have little knowledge of government or international affairs.*

"Stop that, you know better!" Grandma says. "Just continue doing what you are doing and great change will come."

Whoa, great change. From whom... To what? What will change?

"Great change needs to come from the people who are ready and they will make history by going first and bringing back the power of love."

Wow! Could it really be that simple to do? "I bet the naysayers will jump all over that one," I quip. "I feel kind of embarrassed that I even have to write a book on something so obvious, Grandma. I mean, love, when I mention it to people, they just say how silly it is and that it can't be used to try to solve world problems."

She smiles. "Well, people need to learn this now. They just don't know and it's because they rarely use it themselves. Don't take it personally; at the moment they have no idea that their resistance is part of the situation. More than ever, our world really needs this. So much has happened and it's time to band together to solve problems, because there are a lot of them. But this will only work if we learn to truly love ourselves first."

"Wait. I thought you said we are supposed to learn to love others first. I am so confused."

"Dear child, what you will come to know from the loving of others is in fact true self-love."

"To me, it seems backwards," I stubbornly insist. "At the native sweat lodge that I visit, we are told to put ourselves first so that we can be our best to help others."

"I am not talking about catering to and serving other people's material needs," she retorts. "I am talking about sending them invisible love and positive energy. That's all I am asking you to do, and when you send it, it requires nothing else at all."

"How do we do that?"

"Use a deep intention. You intend — on purpose — to send them invisible love."

"That sounds easy, Grandma."

"No, it's not easy at all," she chuckles. "For example, think of somebody that you're not getting along with right now."

So I do. I close my eyes and take a deep breath and visualize a specific person who constantly gets on my nerves. I hold that thought in my imagination for a few seconds.

"How does that feel?" she asks.

"Well, I can literally feel some kind of sensation in my heart and neck area and my stomach feels rumbly."

Grandma nods yes. "Now pay closer attention to those feelings that are going on inside your body. Close your eyes and really observe them. Feel them. They have different sensations; you need to start paying attention to them now and try to separate them from each other. Notice where in your body the emotions are being stored. Once you've grasped the feelings, acknowledge them and imagine giving that person a gift box filled with invisible love while you feel that way about them."

Chapter 5

be.come

"Okay," I say. "But why do you keep calling it invisible love? We all know that love is invisible."

"Because it's a way of practicing conceptualizing that it's an actual thing," she delicately explains. "Don't default on love all of the time. That means don't just let it come to you when it decides to come, intend to give it out, just like you do with hate. Send people love gift boxes."

"Okay, Grandma, this is getting a little too girly-sounding for me. I understand the gift part, but I don't want all this sugar-coated fluff. What will male readers have to say about this way of visualizing it?"

"Don't assume anything. And quite frankly, the men might actually be better at this than the women, in my opinion. Men can be better at stepping out, doing things differently and not worrying about judgment. It just doesn't look the same for a man versus a woman."

"What? Love doesn't look the same for a man as it does for a woman? Grandma, that sounds very sexist."

"No, it's not meant to be; it's the truth. But you keep missing my point. Love can look many ways, but it only feels one way and that's good, pure and undeniable. True love feels like no other feeling in the world; that's how we know what it is. I am going to teach you how to access it whenever you want."

"Okay, Grandma, let's back up, please. Clarify something for me: the expression of love can be very different, but the feeling of it is unique and undeniable?"

"Yes."

"Okay, check. I am with you. Now what?"

"Love is the opposite feeling of hate, so when you are feeling rage, jealousy or hate you are obviously not feeling love."

"Grandma! That's common sense!"

"Are you ready? If so, I am going to talk to you about the next phase of love, but you need to be paying attention."

"Okay, I promise I will," I say excitedly.

"Are you really ready, Birdie?"

"Yes, Grandma, I am."

"Love is a vibration."

"What?"

"A vibration. It's energy. It's an emotion. Emotions are all made up of energy and different vibrations."

"Okay," I say, with a stunned face.

"Let's talk about music," she unexpectedly suggests.

Oh god, I think, forgetting that she can read my every thought and see my rolling eyes. *I thought we were talking about love, now you want to talk about music?*

"Birdie, love and music go together. How many musicians play from their heart?"

"Well, I don't know anything about music but I am guessing it's most of them."

"What makes a famous song?"

I reply with a guess: "Probably because the piece is different, unique, and makes people feel a certain way."

"Exactly," she says, "music is made from love; it's the main ingredient. A song with no heart is just words. Imagine a violin sitting on a floor in an opened case. How does it sound?"

"Like nothing; it has no sound."

"Understand?"

I nod to prod her to keep going.

She continues: "What if a random little boy walked over to that violin and picked it up and started playing? What would it sound like?"

Chapter 5

"Terrible, I am sure; all screechy and sharp."

"Now imagine a world-class master violinist picking it up and playing it; what would that sound like?"

"Probably amazing."

She nods.

"Okay, Grandma, I am sure that you have something really intelligent to wrap that up with right?"

Sounding exceptionally poised and confident, she says, "The true professional in anything has learned to play, create and win from and with love. Love is the creator of the sound and the musician. How well they play is a complete reflection of the vibration of love they used to create it. It is divine essence; no logical thoughts or explanation can describe it any other way. So really love what you do always, and if you don't love it, don't do it. Love with all your heart and be willing to go first."

begin to be.

"Seriously, that's it? Now we are all supposed to be experts in love, Grandma?"

"No," she says simply, "I wanted you to have a base understanding of what love feels like, looks like and sounds like. It's just that, the base."

Now what, I ask?

Sedona
part 2

chapter 6

liberation from the past;
the healing continues; be.coming…

Chapter 6

I am sure that none of the other writers in the room have a clue that so much energetic intelligence is moving around inside of me. It's her. I can see her, feel her. I am channeling my grandma. Actually, in this moment it feels like some other guides are pointing out Grandma's thoughts to me. She does, however, nod and agree with them frequently.

I begin to clue in that she and I are supposed to work out the details of this book and the others are there to cheer me on. Their role is to show me that there are many more beings on the other side helping me and guiding me and encouraging me to be open to whomever might step forward to give me a message. It is almost like I have an army of guides, each one with a different role to play or task to give me.

In this strange and magical space in Sedona, so many memories come back to me. I sit and remember the way Grandma always watched over us.

I remember the way Grandma never spoke badly of anyone or anything around me. She always made sure I felt special. I used to tease her all the time about me being her favourite grandchild. There were ten grandchildren and I was sure I could win the title of the favourite — I just had to stealthily get her to say it. Over the years I would repeatedly ask, "Grandma, I am your favourite grandchild, right?" She would always smile and say, "You are all my favourites." But in my heart, I knew that I had a special place in hers. I thought for sure one day I would be able to trick her into admitting that I was indeed by far her favourite.

She made sure each and every one of us had our freezers full of baking and our beds adorned with her colourful homemade quilts. The amazing thing about the quilts was that they were sewn on a hundred-year-old Raymond high-armed sewing machine that was given to her by her Czechoslovakian mother-in-law on her wedding day. Always giving to others — that's just who she was.

I especially loved the times that Grandma would teach us kids how to make homemade bread, and in the process of us goofing off with it, it would land on the floor several times. She giggled and allowed us to over-work it to extremes. I think she liked to pretend not to notice. The dirtier the bread, the more jam we got to eat with it!

When I was really young, about six years old, Grandma would dance with me. She tried to teach me to two-step to Hank Williams but both of us just laughed and laughed because I couldn't figure out what to do with my feet. Since my grandparents were so poor we would decorate an otherwise bare Charlie Brown Christmas tree with popcorn and thread. Back then, Grandma and Grandpa were probably drunk most of the time. But you could still feel the love.

There was never a time in my life when I didn't feel that love. But we lived in a dangerous place. Each house on either side of Grandma's was occupied by a pedophile.

The house on the right was a cute little white house with bright blue trim, a short white picket fence and matching white shutters. The yard was full of flower gardens. I remember the daisies — lots and lots of daisies among all of the other random mixes of beautiful flowers. An old man by the name of Jerry lived there alone. He was about 80 years old and had medium-length thin white hair and was bald on the top. He walked hunched over, probably from many years of tending to his magnificent garden. He often wore blue or grey trousers and a white t-shirt with suspenders. He always waved over the fence to my grandparents, appearing to be so gentle and sweet.

One day he offered me some candy from a container that he had on his front porch. "Come on over for a candy, little girl," he slyly suggested. I shook my head because I felt afraid but he continued to insist, beckoning for me to come see him. Finally I broke down and walked over. He

Chapter 6

walked towards his front door and stepped right into his kitchen, inviting me in.

My body trembled with fear. Something inside was telling me not to go in, but I didn't listen to it. However, upon entering I announced that I didn't want the candy anymore and abruptly stopped in my tracks and ran back home as fast as I could.

But that wasn't the last time he invited me over for a candy and it wasn't the last time I accepted his invitation. It would be a time that I would never — could never — forget.

The neighbour to the left was my grandma's brother-in -law, so visits to his house happened far more often. This house was also full of drunken welfare recipients and everyone knew Grandma's brother-in-law was a child molester. Horrifically, everyone, including my grandma, looked the other way and did nothing about it. She did grumble about him and make subtle statements about his antics, but she didn't seem to do anything to truly make a difference. I was lucky though — my experiences with him were not completely traumatic. Unfortunately others in my family could not say the same thing.

Despite everything, my grandma was one of the very few people in my world who I felt truly loved me and actually participated in my life. When I slept at my own home I had lots of nightmares. I would sleepwalk often. I would wake up under beds or even in unfilled bathtubs or at the bottoms of staircases. These were likely exterior symptoms of what was going on inside me. I was being sexually abused, witnessing drug and alcohol abuse and violence, and experiencing emotional neglect from both of my parents. That was my everyday environment.

Nobody in my immediate family ever noticed that anything was wrong or just how much I hurt on the inside. As a little girl, all I ever wanted to do was to make people happy. Don't get me wrong — there were indeed some good times in my life. I had friends and got to play with dolls and catch frogs with my cousins at family functions. But the urge to please was always with me.

Chapter 6

be.come

Consequently I would turn to my dreams to escape reality. That's how I chose to survive it all. When I was four years old and had nightmares, I would lie in my bed feeling terrified. I felt like I had nobody whom I could talk to or be with. I always felt like nobody understood me, and that I never fit in with most people in my family. I was the little lost sheep. So I would turn to my imagination and create little stories or visions of what my life could look like if I was allowed to make my own choices.

I sometimes would spend an entire day building a script with characters and scenes. I have to admit that most of them included me having lots of money, swimming pools and diamonds. When I went to sleep I could be and do anything I wanted and nobody could laugh at my experiences. They were mine and that was important to me. As long as I kept them to myself nobody could take them away. Through all of the dreams, I kept hope. I truly believed that anything was possible and wondered why other people couldn't see the potential for more in life. To me it appeared absolutely possible. I knew I could have it all somehow.

Chapter 6

When I wasn't dreaming, I spent my childhood pleasing others. When I tried to express myself, others laughed or said I was being stupid. I would often daydream of being rich and living on the top of Bear Mountain, which is not really a mountain, but more like a large hill on the edge of the small city we lived in. When I was young, Bear Mountain was where all of the so-called rich people lived, and being rich was important to me. I specifically wanted a large glass house with big chandeliers, complete with a handsome blonde-haired, blue-eyed husband who was also an excellent father. I constantly repeated this particular daydream.

Now, washed over with years of childhood memories, sitting silently at the writer's retreat in Sedona while other writers scribbled around me, I use my inner voice to speak to my grandma.

"Grandma, I have learned to manifest most of what I need in life and I think I owe it all to my ability to dream.

Chapter 6
be.come

But how would I teach someone else to do this if they weren't already a dreamer? I think that it might be hard for people to allow themselves to dream. In my experience many people avoid dreaming and run in the other direction toward logic, so that they don't get accused of living with their heads in the clouds."

"There is nothing to run from," she says, in a deep and divine tone. "You'd only be running from yourself and that's pointless. You cannot grow and become *how* you want to be. So take a deep breath right now and exhale.

"Understand that you are actually learning how to be you and that it is meant to be an adventure full of love and joy. You deserve it and are at a place where you can go anywhere you want. This is your guide if you choose to follow yourself through the process and commit to *yourself* on all levels. Allow some things to show up that may *feel* less than joyous or maybe even a bit strange and trust this process will guide you to the right place. That place is *you*. I am merely trying to guide you back to *you*.

Chapter 6

"So let's get started," she says firmly. "Who are you? So what? What does your report card even look like? Nobody cares in this exact moment anyway!

"It's all about shedding the supposed you and learning about the true you — the essence of who you are — and then getting back to that for the rest of your time here on earth. Let's understand something, Birdie: there is only a certain amount of clock time left for you on this planet, so wouldn't you enjoy knowing you and living a stress-free life, creating whatever you want?"

"Yes," I respond seriously.

"Then break free of conformity! This book we are writing is not a lottery ticket or a fast track, it's just not. It's the road back to you — by you — so enjoy it. So many people are still searching outside themselves for happiness, fulfillment or acceptance. Not being loved or understood is a huge part of life and contributes to so much of what we create ourselves to be right now. Many people feel life can be crushing, paralyzing or debilitating. But what if I told you that that's not even possible? Would you throw this book into the corner and shout out, 'Grandma doesn't have a clue!'?"

"Grandma," I say, blown away by all I am hearing from her, "when I am manifesting my true desires I have learned how to reach out to my higher self, but not that long ago I had no idea how to make things really happen. I mean, I did make lots happen, but it was all luck of the draw and willy-nilly. I was never really certain what might show up once I sent out my request to the big guys." I point up to Heaven; as if she doesn't know which big guys I am referring to. "I have come to realize that I am here to learn right now. I almost always get an answer from guides when I request one, but sometimes it shows up much later than I had wanted. Amazingly, more often than not something so much better happens in the end."

"That's how it all happens," she chortles. "Everything shows up right on time. You don't get the new car or the diploma before it's the right time. Once you have set your intention, or asked your guides or higher self for help, it starts to come. Once you have established your needs and desires, a manifestation requires some sort of action. The smallest step can move mountains in the big picture, but you do have to take some sort of step if you want results. Growth and healing show up when the time is right and opportunities present themselves to you. It's up to you if you choose to take them or not. The right time for you can only be determined by you. Is it now or is it later?"

"Thank you, Grandma. I love you for that. It makes so much sense to me. I guess I have never really thought about the fact that I may have let the opportunity pass me by from time to time."

"It's true that many people experience paralyzing thoughts every day and that they often believe it's the other person's fault. They feel the other person may be ruining their life or challenging them on some level. But that's not real. Let's discuss that... it's like this: if your spouse is always angry or violent with you, is he making you feel less than worthy or are you choosing to feel that way? It's true, he would be considered to be behaving badly and clearly reacting to something going on inside of his heart but there is no way at all he could *make* you feel one particular feeling. Those are your feelings and whichever one you choose to carry determines what the result of the situation will be."

I mull over her words and then say, "I know that, Grandma, but what happens when I do legitimately feel angry, mad, sad or jealous? I mean, are you asking me to fake a feeling just to create or manifest the things that I want?"

"You could choose to feel lonely, angry, revengeful or sad but ultimately you choose the feeling you want to experience based on the actions of the other person. In the same situation many people would pick a different feeling. Why would one person feel sad while another might choose anger?"

"Hmmm, I am not sure where you might be trying to take me with all of this, Grandma. All I want to know is how does all of this affect my ability to create what I want in life?"

"You see," she explains, "the feelings you experience as a result of someone else's behaviour are completely your choice and not theirs. I am not in any way condoning bad behaviour and don't want to discount your feelings at all. In fact the opposite is what I am after: *feel* your feelings and recognize how you currently respond to different peoples' behaviour. You might not even realize it but you might be developing the same reactions as them over time. What if you could actually choose the opposite thoughts and feelings in the same situation? You can. What would it look like if you chose understanding and sent love to that person instead of choosing hurt, anger and sadness? Feelings are important indicators to help us change the direction of any situation that we are dealing with."

"So if I have this right, I am supposed to simply observe myself and the reactions I create based on other peoples' actions for now? And if at all possible, just consider how using another feeling to respond might change the result?"

"Thoughts are just that: thoughts. All of them are changeable. So if a woman decided to change her thoughts about her feelings around her lacklustre marriage, what could that look like? All thoughts are changeable in an instant, but you must know that it doesn't mean that the feelings are. Feelings and thoughts work together. The human spirit and body are the most divine creations of all things. How do we change a feeling? And do we even want to? What is the purpose of feelings and how can we use these natural tools to grow and become? You are being asked to commit to learning and understanding your feelings so people don't remain paralyzed or stifled anymore."

"Fine, I can change a thought, but not a feeling? I thought you just said that I could change a feeling too."

"This is the process, Birdie. It's called life and we are all going through similar human events with one person or another. Relationships are never perfect. That's because they were set up as lessons from above so that we could all come to know our true selves and pass down this inherent knowledge to those next in line.

"We are here in the physical world creating and interpreting all things differently and think many different things and feel countless emotions. What a gift! Hard sometimes, you say? Yes, for a bit, but only a short bit, then you will come to know your own energy and thank the universe for different situations that start to appear in your life. Many want to now know themselves but get trapped in fear of what they might actually find. So for now, *think* about changing a thought and only observe your feelings.

"Birdie, it's like a big pot of gold at the end of a rainbow. This book will be beautifully written and 110 times better than you could have ever imagined it to be. I promise, you will start magnificently attracting wonderful things into your life. Some will seem good and some will appear bad, but each one, no matter how hard, will just be small lessons in becoming you. When playing a game you can't get to the finish line right at the start — you actually have to go through each step. You can't cheat to win. It's a methodical game of seeing, feeling and sometimes strategizing your next move. You do have to think, but you win this game thinking with your heart!" Grandma laughs happily.

"*Think* with your heart?" I repeat. "Observe your feelings so that you can decide to change them later? Why later,

Chapter 6

be.come

Grandma? I just realized we never finished that conversation! You said thoughts were changeable in an instant but feelings weren't.

"Throw me a bone, Gram, what am I missing?"

"Becoming is a process," she explains. "So if you don't want to process or grow, simply close the book for now. This lesson is not optional, it's required. Changing your feelings is absolutely possible; people always do it. But what it needs is more time. Honour yourself and your true feelings. Don't judge them. Simply observe, become aware, accept them and then your reactions will shift over time.

"Birdie, most people know that thoughts can be inaccurate at times. We can take a molehill and build it into a mountain if we are coming from a victim position. Once we realize our thoughts are not serving us, we can choose to try the feeling of acceptance on that same issue. Again, it takes time and practice to learn a new way of doing things, but the situation will absolutely shift. However you create it is the result of your *thinking* and *feelings,* combined with the actions you take."

"Why didn't you just say it needed more time then, Grandma? That would have been a lot simpler, wouldn't it?"

"Birdie, this book is creating itself to show up when it is needed and to whom it is needed by. Some will keep it; some will re-gift it or use it as a door-stop. There will be a precise time that people will need this book and it's up to you to ask yourself if now is that time for you. Listen and respect the answer that you hear. So there is only one time; you get to decide when that is for you, but I will warn you, there is no halfway. I mean no halfway back to yourself. You will get there over time if you continue on this path, but if you don't, you will remain not who you are at all, forever. It's your decision."

Grandma's
wisdom

chapter 7

wisdom gathered along the way;
instructions for readers…

Chapter 7

be.come

After Sedona, my life continues to transform. Much of what Grandma has taught me about love and the process of be.coming comes to fruition in my life. This chapter describes these transformations and how Grandma's wisdom deepened in my life.

finding a tribe

A friend once told me that when you start shifting, you will experience a friend-ectomy. What is that? It's when you start to shift and evolve, and some of your current friends may not be as present in your life and may fall by the wayside for a bit. Some of them come back in good time and some don't. But do not worry.

Two things happen: the first is that beautiful new people start showing up everywhere. Be open to that. The great thing about that is they don't know the *old you* and so it's really easy to practice your new true self with them. It's easier because you can let go of the past blocks, feelings or guards. Even if it doesn't always feel good because these new people don't quite understand you, this process creates a space where you get to try out your new skills. Understand that these people are in a state of process too and were assigned to your journey for one reason or another. That's the exciting part: the gradual unweaving of one of life's mysteries. Look deeper, see what you can find, and learn.

Over the last six years since Grandma passed, I have been guided into a whole new version of myself. At random, I have been so fortunate to meet over a dozen different beautiful lady friends who were all experiencing similar things, wanting to learn more about themselves and the energetic side of life. Interestingly, they started coming from all over.

In no time at all, I had more friends than I had ever had before at one time. They all were delighted to discover that other people in our small town wanted to learn more about themselves on a deeper level. Each friend met the other and before long we had a sort of tribe. Each person contributes stories, fears and dreams, and offers valuable tools and resources.

Over the last few years these relationships have helped me to learn some of the greatest lessons of my life. These friends won't let me get rid of them with my invisible scissors, no matter how ugly the situation gets. I admit I still carry those scissors around and I'm still tempted to use them from time to time. When I no longer want people in my life, I pull my scissors out and cut the umbilical cord to that person in hopes of releasing them from my world. Goodbye, issue or friendship. Goodbye to any pain before it shows up and I have to feel it. How smart is that? I am a genius… or at least I thought I was.

But when you have these people who continue to love you even when you are a grumpy asshole, you need to pause. If they accept you truly as you are and are willing to let you be who you really are, with any imperfections you might have been handed when you were sent to this lifetime, hold onto those friends.

Without each one of my friends, my story would look so different. I am certain that Grandma went and hand-picked each one of them for me so that I could learn what I needed to learn about myself and finally understand how using essence instead of ego could make my life so much richer.

essence or ego

When you want to create or change something in your life you have to know that coming from essence instead of ego will make the process so much better. You can build anything you want from ego; I know because I have done it many times. However, it's not all that fun sometimes, and doesn't bring as much joy as one might hope. Learning how to manifest from true essence allows everything to come to you so effortlessly and joyously. Generally the gifts or opportunities that do show up are far better than you could have ever hoped for. The reason is because you are not controlling the outcome and disrupting the natural flow of your energy and law of attraction.

Nothing worthy happens until it is actually the right time. What that means for me is that you have to start by telling the universe what you want and how you want it. Simply ask for it with gratitude and love. It will show up for you when your essence is completely aligned with and true to yourself and your feelings. You must love yourself and the other people involved if you want it to be a genuine success.

Grandma said it best. Nothing really good happens until that moment of reaching a climax of true love in any given situation. It's all in the universal divine setup. Once again: nothing. This is a very important rule. Your guides will bring you everything you desire once you become completely in love with the thought, idea and people whom you need to help you move triumphantly forward through the process.

We all say we want to be rich or have more money, but what do we do to be rich? Not a lot, actually. Even when saving or investing money, most people have some level of stress towards it. They don't really believe the returns will come back in the way that they desire. The fact is, most people don't feel worthy of being rich, so they can't actually create wealth.

If you truly want financial freedom, you need to focus on getting down to your core beliefs on the issue. Look at all the fine details of who you are. Look at all the positive financial steps you take and decide how you want to go forward. Building quality relationships with people who do know and care about money should be your first step, then it's up to you to take an action to get that momentum going. It can start with just five dollars. Your objective is to love that five dollars and believe it will bring good to you and many others. You must believe you are worth more, then take action to grow it into more than five dollars. So many people live in default mode. They say, "Well, whatever happens, happens." They rarely set intentions or commit to themselves from essence.

Chapter 7

be.come

Lots of times opportunities come in interesting packages and you just have to be willing to see them. Spend some time looking at everyday things and extract the fine details out of these situations. Getting out of ego and into essence means accepting all that is, and loving it for what it is. Sending love to whomever and whatever, even when you're angry, jealous or sad, helps you to shift yourself and the energy around the given situation.

Let me be clear: it does not mean being fake. I don't want you to discount your own real feelings at all. It means recognizing them, feeling them and thanking them for showing up so you can learn something more about yourself. Then you ask yourself, "How can I make this better by coming from essence?"

It's a win-win tool. It has always worked for me since I started using it several years ago. I will admit that I don't use it 100 per cent of the time because I forget. Plus, sometimes I want to be angry, disappointed or upset. I guess there's a part of me that feels like I still want that energy in my life from time to time. But what I also know to be true is that once I recognize it, I can shift my energy at any given moment to make things better. When I get off track, I remind myself or reach out to my friends to help me focus.

When something really sucks, it's an opportunity for you to practice using and exploring essence. From my experience, it takes a lot of practice. I have been going at it for at least three years now and I have to tell you that I have seen significant changes in my life from it. Because of it, the ripple effect grows larger and larger amongst the people in my life.

the process of creation

Many people are learning how to tap into the vibrations of love. They are learning to enjoy that conversation with themselves and with others. This new knowledge of who they have become creates an opportunity to live life in a way they have never known before. They can spread that knowledge to family and friends to create a much larger circle of life and love. Imagine the vibrational web expanding outwards across the world as thousands and thousands of people transform themselves.

Chapter 7

be.come

Creating who you are is both easy and hard. It completely depends on your emotional and mental state and how much practice you are willing to put into it. Being seen becomes a reality. Nobody has ever actually died from being seen. In one particular meditation that I completed with a friend I heard the words: "Teach them how to be seen by going first." It's your heart that people want to see and feel, and not your ego.

The steps are a process, a process in which you make a special discovery about yourself. You will begin to notice the lessons but not know how to proceed through emotions or solve the problems that go with them. You will *see* the problem and *feel* the feelings and will be stumped as to how to process the occasionally difficult emotions you are having. You may experience guilt over having them and not know what to do with them.

At this point you should congratulate yourself for how far you've already come. You can now actually *see* the circumstance and *feel* the emotion that you chose to attach to it. This is a big deal. You must continue to practice the rest of the steps. Many are not even aware that this is a *thing* or a process, but it is at this exact moment that you need to realize that you have made it. That's the hardest part: to allow yourself to recognize what it is and have the willingness to go forward and step into whatever that may look and feel like so you can alter the outcome of your life.

Always remember that your friends are also entitled to their own progression strategies. Honour that. They are in their own place and their timing may be different than yours. Process that.

The benefits to allowing new people in your life include all the new opportunities that present themselves to you. The opportunities that start showing up for you will floor you — in a good way, of course. As long as you are making decisions from a place of love every day, you will be able to accept the things you want when they show up. To take them or not to take them will be your only question. You will also choose the emotions that you attach to them. All are wonderful and acceptable, not good or bad, because now you are in a place where you get to witness the creation of *you*. The real divine you whom you were born to be. Creation becomes a choice — your choice. It's interesting, fun and exciting! Even the ugly stuff becomes a chance to reflect on yourself and how you will choose to step through the ugliness.

Throughout this process you might revisit old relationships and associated feelings. You can ask yourself: "What was I feeling anyway? What was I seeing and feeling and how do I feel about it now?" It's almost never about the other person. Usually, it's actually a reflection of all that's going on inside of you. Over time the energy changes because nothing can remain constant forever.

let's practice creating right now

Close your eyes. Take a deep breath all the way into your belly. Bring the oxygen deeply into your chest, into the sides of your body and down into your belly. Hold for the count of four and very slowly release and exhale with sound. Now repeat. Do it again and again until you *feel* that your body has relaxed somewhat.

Think of someone who you have been annoyed with. What was that about? Why did you choose the feeling that you chose? Envision that person in your imagination and replay the situation over and over in your mind for a few minutes. How did that *feel*? Was it difficult? Were you angry, sad, mad, disappointed or let down? Did you experience trust issues or was your heart broken? Right now, try to notice what is happening in your body as a result of those thoughts. Can you feel any tension or hurt in a particular physical place? Take another deep breath and exhale completely.

When thinking of this person who let you down, can you feel anything in your stomach, neck, heart or bowels? Are you tightening them up, getting gas or feeling any kind of pain? If so, that's your body reacting to the emotions you have chosen to attach to that circumstance. Common effects of emotional stress can cause headaches, muscle tension or pain, fatigue, change in sex drive, an upset stomach, and sleep problems.

Congratulate yourself. You just became aware of exactly how damaging these types of thoughts and emotions can be to your body. I bet you never thought for a second that a difficult relationship with another person was harming your body and wreaking havoc on your insides.

People who manage stress well are very good at moving the energy and hard feelings outward instead of inward. Although some people reactively move the feelings outward in an aggressive manner, it's so much easier on everyone to practice the action of consciously and peacefully moving the energy outward. After practicing this you will get better and stressful people or situations will not upset you so much. You will feel disappointed, angry and resentful less and less.

If, on the other hand, you didn't notice anything happening in your body when you summoned these negative feelings, you might be so disconnected with yourself that you have no idea of the damage that could be going on. It's percolating and will show up in the future, so it's time to trust that this book has landed in your hands for a reason. It is likely a message for you to slow down and start taking a look at your body and emotions.

If the same stressful, aggravating or annoying situation presented itself again would you change the way you handled yourself? Would you now feel motivated to make change for at least the sake of your body?

Of course it all sounds like a good idea, but *how* do we actually do it?

If you asked that question, you're right where you need to be. You've just made another shift. You are now aware of your thoughts and are asking questions that are attached to your body. Even though you don't know what to do about it in this moment, that's okay. Your body is the vehicle that takes you from here to there. Your feelings help create your body and the body doesn't lie. I believe that what is happening on the outside of your body is a reflection of what is going on inside.

The abuse and neglect I endured as a child caused me to suffer from fight-or-flight syndrome for several years. Once I finally recognized how reactive and stressed I was — and more importantly, *why* I was — it all started to change. That took four years for me to recognize. But once I did, in an instant there was a shift. I had to learn some major life lessons and get in touch with the feelings *emotionally* and *physically* before I could progress with it.

During my fight-or-flight stage, I gained about 25 or 30 pounds. It was so unlike me but no matter what I did, I couldn't shake it. I am now sure that this was happening to me so that I would learn to understand emotions and all that comes with them. For example, weight is a form of protection and it came to me with my feelings of fear around the new changes in my life.

Everything I am telling you is actually common sense. But until you can *see* it and *feel* it you won't be able to change anything. When you do you get to go to the next step of the process, some of you will experience the *feel* part first while others will be able to *see* things more clearly. This is about discovering your own senses and which ones you naturally use first. The order does not matter. What matters is that emotionally and physically you are starting to understand a little bit more about yourself and know that you do have the tools inside of you to make change. And you've had them all along.

Being aware is like looking into a mirror and seeing what's really there. Some people dislike looking into mirrors because they feel and think things about themselves they don't like. It's perfectly normal and we all do it at some point. The second step is to go beyond the *mind and feel* of your feelings. This takes *time* to develop because you have experiences and false beliefs to unlearn. We have to respect the *time* it will take to commit to this process. It's just that: a process. People learn life at various speeds. There are certainly no hard and fast timelines. It's about being willing to expand yourself. Becoming anything is a process.

The process and vibration of energy with which you choose to express yourself is the thread of the needle that binds your story together. Every moment of any situation can vibrate faster, slower, denser, lighter, thicker or thinner depending on which emotion you choose to attach to it.

Energy is constant and always in motion, so you have the ability and the right to move it, change it or accept it in any moment.

Imagine for a moment that you are in an argument with your partner or child. You want some time to yourself but the other person demands your attention. Insisting on getting some personal space, you lose your temper, freak out and tell them to get lost. What do you think the vibration of that scenario would be? Obviously it would be dense, heavy energy and cause some emotional turmoil for the other involved parties.

But what if you decided that you wanted to change that outcome while still securing the time and space you desire? How could this scenario be changed to alter the energetic outcome? I am sure this will seem absolutely obvious and simple, but have you ever actually pulled yourself back from a difficult situation to see how it all played out before? When you learn how to do that it makes new situations easier to work through because you have become aware of your energy and the energy of others. You know that you have the power to change every-thing in your life if you truly want to.

As it turns out, sometimes it seems that our soul doesn't actually want to change the vibration even when it's heavy and dense. As long as you are aware of making this choice, it's perfectly fine. However, what you need to know is that threads of that event, person, place or thing will also vibrate at that speed or density and living with the results will be part of your story. How you choose to deal with all that vibrates from your choices is how you end up writing the story of your life.

the final lesson

chapter 8

a sword fight at the finish line;
a life's calling unveiled…

Chapter 8
be.come

It's April 12, 2016. After almost six years of constant learning about myself, I am happy and relieved to realize that the completion of this book is signaling to me that this leg of my journey is nearly complete. But after 30 pounds, the loss of friends and family members, and a deep search for myself, I encounter one more sword fight two feet in front of the finish line.

In the last few years someone entered my life for what seemed like no reason at all. I tried to like this person and find my way with her, but I just couldn't. It was like I was the water and she was the oil. Energetically we could not mix or understand each other, but I kept bumping into her all over the place. I found her exterior appearance to be beautiful and felt she was extremely talented, yet some indescribable essence was in the air around her. I could feel her resistance, yet at the same time I could feel her interest in and professional respect for me.

After several uncomfortable and unusual encounters, I just decided to let it go. Whatever was happening energetically was not mine; it was hers. Still, I wondered if I could have been wrong. Maybe I was making a big mistake judging her? So I asked myself to feel the feelings that were taking place, to witness them and be honest to myself about what they looked like.

She reached out to speak with me on a few occasions but the last time it felt like she energetically sliced me in the back with a knife full of jealousy and envy. It sounds totally arrogant, but I could feel it. The signs and psychic messages were coming at me from every direction and I couldn't ignore them any longer. Or could I? The messages were telling me that I was a mirror of her. I was able to do things that she could do professionally. That was causing concern for her.

Chapter 8

At no time was I ever unpleasant with her. I even offered to help her professionally a couple of times, so I was somewhat angry and disappointed. My feelings were just plain hurt.

I started to pull out my invisible scissors once again in order to cut her loose, but this time as I raised the scissors I heard a voice. I looked at my hand and saw what I was about to do for the first time. It wasn't my first time using the scissors; it was just my first time seeing the consequences.

"Birdie," said Grandma, "this is your final lesson and what you have come to know shall be revealed now. Think before you react, listen to what your body is saying and believe in yourself. You have the power."

Ugggh, this pisses me right off! I want to be mad. I want to win. I want to poke this jealous person in the eye.

Some years ago a medicine man told me that I would suffer from the jealousy and envy of others a lot in my life. He said these experiences would surely provide one of my greatest life lessons. Not because I was out-of-this-world amazing, but because we all come here to live and learn and this was, for whatever reason, what I had to live through and learn.

I never did anything to hurt this person. I gifted her, and tried my best to expose her to the people she wanted to know, and yet I was cheated by her dislike for me. Amidst my emotions, I try to repeat these words in my head: "Send her love." Just as Grandma once taught me.

This timing feels terrible. I am so close to finishing this book on the tight deadline and now I have one more stupid lesson to learn? Haven't I done enough? I help people all day long as much as possible. I give them healing and advice and channel their dead ones through my physical body. I would give anyone the shirt off my back if they needed it, and you have one more lesson for me?

I am so mad at God. I know he is there with Grandma. I can feel Him. I know this is His fault, not hers. Screw you!

Chapter 8

be.come

One more lesson from this nobody person. I barely know her. I have no idea why she showed up into my world. I don't appreciate how she is trying to block me from accomplishing what I need to do psychically and energetically. And now I can't just get rid of her?

"She's nobody to me!" I shout out.

Then I start asking myself if she really is a *nobody*. Why does it hurt me that she doesn't seem to like me? I can't come up with an answer and nobody from above is saying anything either. In my frustration I stomp around my living room trying to make sense of this crappy situation and then I hear God say, "I have assigned her to you."

"What?" I say indignantly. "God, are you serious? You jerk! Thanks! For all I have done for you, all the people I try to help and events that I create, you give me this? Your timing sucks! I just want to finish this damn book and get back to living life and taking care of my family and business."

"It was your final lesson," he says. "And once you realize that you can overcome it you will have the power to do anything."

I feel alone. I'm sure I am being punished for something that I must have done. It all feels so real in this moment, so intense and hard. Seconds later, there is a knock at the door.

It's my friend Lisa. She's popped over to practice her recent training at a meditative breathing program that she just completed. After all the pressure and the emotional rollercoaster of writing this book, I had accepted her offer to teach me. I couldn't wait to clear some of my emotional blocks and I knew that I needed serious help to push the book one last step to completion.

During the practice, I lay on the floor with my hands beside my body and a small pillow under my upper back meant to help open my heart wall. I am lying on a feather duvet with a pillow under my head. The heat is cranked in the house and I feel very relaxed and safe.

I start by executing a specific breathing pattern that she initiates and directs me to follow while listening to some incredible meditation music. This pattern goes on for an hour or so; it feels like forever and I struggle a lot to keep to her guided rhythm. My breathing is fast and fiery. My arms start to tingle right away.

After the first hour of lying in the meditative breathing arrangement, my arms begin to very slowly lift off the floor and move towards each other, shaking. My fingers form an unusual pattern and lock. I am unable to physically move them. Since I have been mediating for about five years now, I don't find this development frightening.

In this meditative time-space, I am completely able to have logical discussions with myself. I ask myself, "What could be going on here? Why are my arms rising and why are they shaking so badly?" My right hand and arm begin to flap in a gentle repeating pattern with my wrist flicking sharply like wing tips.

I completely surrender, breathing in the pattern directed by Lisa. She continues to hold space for me, circulating a pendulum over me to work my energy and keep me balanced. She touches my body in a safe massage-like way to activate different chakras. Her kind gentle voice tells me that everything is as it should be, and I am doing well.

The room is filled with a great amount of trust and respect and I feel remarkable but heavily weighted at the same time. My emotions are swirling all over the place. My arms continue to slowly rise and shake but now it feels like somebody has put something in each of my hands. I feel God around me. I see Him in front of my face and ask Him what He has put in my hands.

My body is trembling, tears are rolling out of my eyes, and my heart is pounding. I feel as though I am the only one who has to endure deep darkness. I know I am totally connected to God and that I am receiving a gift, but just what could it be?

Chapter 8

I ask again, "God, what is this gift you have for me?"

"I have given you the gift of courage," He finally says. "That is what you came to this lifetime to be: courageous. It seems difficult right now, but when you get to a certain point, it will be so easy."

I continue to lay and repeat His words in my head. I try to comprehend why this is all happening. It seems to be so much greater than me, something like in a movie, but no: everything is very real.

Learning what it takes to have and keep true friendships has been among my greatest life challenges so far. Tears still streaming, I allow my emotions to release and no longer are they stored inside of my body. I can feel my face form the ugly cry: tears, snot and curled lips encapsulate loneliness, judgment and heaviness. I am being seen by one of my most trusted and respected friends — in other words, I am *really* being seen. I can feel that her heart feels mine. There is nothing that can be hidden about me or within me in this moment as I am wide open.

I acknowledge that I am ready for this and that Grandma sent the right friend for the job. But I hear God say that it was He who paired Lisa up with me to help each other through the hard things in life. I thank Him for that gift and can deeply feel my friend's loving energy and her absolute desire for me to completely heal.

I ask God why I have a hard time accepting the fact that many people don't try to become their best selves and that it doesn't appear that they put in as much effort as they could.

"As you now know," God says, "this is your life lesson to learn and that's because you will become a teacher of the experience. That is what you are here to teach, so you must learn it to the core of your being to be able to deliver it to others."

Suddenly, my hands stop shaking and flapping. My arms slowly come together over my head to make the shape of a circle. It is almost as if my body's movements are trying to tell me a story. When my hands connect together above my head, I ask God, "What does all of this mean? What do you want me to know?"

I clearly hear Him say, "The world."

Bling. The bell to end the session rings and I hear Lisa start to guide me back to myself. I feel so light, free and even a bit dizzy. My body is experiencing so much. It is releasing stored-up stress, tension and anger. I can see the face of the woman I was angry with and can now feel my body release her emotionally. I visualize her face shrinking away and wholeheartedly send her invisible love, as I am *feeling* very thankful for the release and experience. After standing up again, I realize that I truly feel nothing but respect for this unnamed challenger and accept her lesson as a gift.

I thank my friend. I am reminded of her gifts and her ability to hold space for me when I need it the most, allowing me to be completely open and vulnerable.

I am finally learning just what I was brought to this earth to do. So many of us just go through the motions of trying to be something or somebody. We do things that will make us look better. We accomplish stuff that will leave our name in the sand in some egotistical way. Or we just coast, not doing anything with any intention at all, living by default.

Later that same day I was struggling to get this book finished and synergistically one of my tribe members, my beautiful friend Shelley, sent me an important message, some words from the author Mandy Hale. It read: "Trust the wait. Embrace the uncertainty. Enjoy the beauty of becoming. When nothing is certain, anything is possible."

I'm in my home office in Dawson Creek, B.C. I'm finishing a manuscript — *this* manuscript. I look at a massive wall of windows and see an overcast day. I smell the intense fragrance of rain about to pour down. The valley is turning from brown to green, denoting springtime is upon us and growth is in the air.

Chapter 8

be.come

I had a visit with my dad and grandfather yesterday and was given a photo of my grandmother's provincial ID card, as she never did get her driver's license. I was thrilled to see her face and name on it as I had received a message a couple of days earlier from her while in meditation. She told me that she personally wanted to write the preface to this book. As she told me this, I realized that adding her signature to the book would be perfect as it would signify that it was her message, not mine. And there it was, on her license.

Everyone who knew her growing up always called my grandmother Doris. Her real name is Adele, or perhaps Adel. Actually there was no official birth certificate and her family often disputed the correct spelling. Over the years, through the drinking days and loss of family members — many due to suicide — nobody could actually decide which one it was. An *e* or no *e* on the end? Her death certificate was labeled with no *e*, but her very own real-life signature includes the *e*.

I reached out to Spirit and asked Grandma how she would like it spelled in this book. She told me, "With no *e* please!" I will honour that and spell it her way as she has nobly requested.

It's amazing how important these details are and what's really in a name. We often don't think about the importance of someone's name until we lose that person. At that time, it's one of the only things we have left that helps us keep their energy alive and known here on earth.

One thing I am starting to acquire now in my mediumship is the ability to hear names from people who have died. That's really exciting because it helps to qualify the details for the person who has requested a reading from me. There have been a few times I have been awakened in the middle of the night by spirits who were literally yelling names at me and giving me messages that I needed to give to their people on this side.

On one occasion I received a message for a professional acquaintance who I am sure would never be open to hearing about spirit and the afterlife. It was his father. He came through to yell his specific first and last name out to me, and with such clarity. Another time the stepfather of a

Chapter 8

be.come

young man who had previously had a session with me wanted his stepson to know he was drinking way too much. He was very concerned. He made sure that he woke me up to tell the young man just how upset he was for not taking his advice seriously.

Both of these father-spirits shouted out their names, almost demanding I do something about it immediately. The first occasion was at approximately 2:00 AM and the other was at about 4:30 AM. I told them both I would do as they asked but to get lost so I could go back to sleep. I won't say this happens all the time, but when it does, I understand how important it is. Not just for the people who are still alive, but for the ones who have crossed over as well, as they feel like they are still guiding and helping their loved ones. They do see everything that we are up to, good or bad.

From my personal experience, I can tell you that they are very much the same on the other side. You don't have to worry about whether they have changed because they haven't. That being said, in a couple of cases, they have shown up better than they were in real life. I would say that that's true for my grandma. She has the same loving energy, but somehow something about her has been taken to another level. It's almost like she found herself over there, receiving the confidence she needed to truly shine. In life she never drove a vehicle and never got her license after crashing into the fence during her first lesson with Grandpa. But now she visits the Canadian Maritimes in my dreams. And who knows where else she's been — she doesn't tell me everything!

With absolute gratitude for my journey, I replay in my mind all the events of the last few years. These friendships, the emotional tribulations, professional shifts and accomplishments have taught me so much about who I am. Each person walks into your life for a reason. You could be learning from them, or you might be growing together because you are at the same emotional place, or maybe you are teaching them something. Often it's a combination of all three. At some point there will be a divide in the road. You may have a short or a long time together, but if it's family, that usually lasts until death.

Death is not really the end, however; in my case it was just the beginning. What was once my greatest fear

Chapter 8

be.come

— losing the most important woman in my life — has metamorphosed into an experience of healing and light. Now that Grandma no longer has a physical presence, her energy remains strong and available to me whenever I call out to her. I have noticed through this process of learning, growing and healing that I don't call out to her as often as I used to. I feel good about that. We should be able to trust ourselves. We need to follow what we know is good and true without constantly relying on advice and confirmation from those people we believe to be wiser than ourselves.

What I have come to know is that it's not always a *give what you get* world, but a *keep who you are* world. They say that you attract the people who reflect you. You attract the ones who are financially, spiritually and morally aligned with you and live by your particular standards, whatever they may be. I guess I do believe that there is some truth to that — it's the law of attraction — but I would also like to add that when you can sense things, vibrationally speaking, the details get more important. You'll notice more deeply that the relationships in your life ebb and flow like a day out on the ocean. Sometimes they are smooth and relaxed, other times they are as aggressive and surprising as a slap in the face. It's up to you to learn how to flow with these changes because each day everyone's vibrations change and they are not meant to be judged or controlled by you. It's not possible to do that anyway. Acceptance of what is has been one of my own greatest life challenges. I love change and am passionate about making the world a better place.

I cannot say I have overcome every obstacle in my life, and I do continue to work on the issue of high expectations of others. Sometimes that's still hard. When I do choose to go back to that place of expectation, I remind myself that I am only human, and will grow and evolve when I have learned exactly what it is I need to know. The lessons always present themselves at precisely the right time, as evolution is always at work, even when it doesn't feel that way.

"Grandma," I say, safe and happy in my home in Dawson Creek, "I want to wholeheartedly thank you for guiding me back to myself. I got off track for the last several years. I was blindly shooting random arrows at an invisible target. I feel fortunate that I have such a supportive husband and children, but without you, Grandma, I am really not sure where I would be. You've taught me about intuition and guidance in a way that no book could have ever done. I feel peaceful most of the time and understand how everything that happens leads to the next phase of life. For that I am thankful."

"Birdie," she says, "Knowing what you know is the way back to peace. For example, now that you have recognized the feeling and admitted to yourself that you have reached the next piece of the puzzle, now what? Feel that. Feel what it feels like to recognize the feeling of thinking something new or knowing something new.

"Find others who are in a similar place so you can share what you have come to know about yourself. Ironically, all the people you will need to help you to get where you are going will start showing up in your life just when you need them. It happened to me up here, but I will tell you that you have to have your eyes open and be willing to share. Once you share, others will share many times, but you have to go first. In going first, you free yourself from carrying the heavy stuff around and you show others that you care enough about yourself to get through it.

"What you don't know yet is that because you open yourself up, even a little, it shows others that it's safe for them to do the same. That's change happening in real time. Just like the old saying, when the student is ready, the teacher will appear."

the beginning

chapter 9

learning to fly…

Chapter 9

be.come

Over the last five or six years since Grandma passed, I have learned to really see my own growth, rebirth and desire for change. I am not at all who I used to be. And when the next book comes I won't be this person either. I don't have to be. The greatest gift that you could give yourself is the permission to become your true self, whenever that feels right for you. This book and the true-life story it tells are a gift that God and Grandma gave to me — to give to you. It's the gift of becoming.

I speak to Grandma now, saying: "Thank you, Grandma, for always showing me unconditional love and teaching me how to love. I am truly grateful for everything you have done for me and for the incredible people in my life. Love never dies."

And she responds, gently saying, "Enjoy the ride and create away. Love, love, love will be the main result of this book. Starting with yourself. You had to start by loving others. But now you must learn to love yourself. If you do, the love for others will follow and be much easier. After all, love flows in circles. It's all the same, no matter whether it's coming to us or through us.

"Remember, when we are pointing the finger at someone else and attaching emotions to that problem, it's actually really about us, not them, and it's time to look inside. If somebody tells us that they don't like something we did, why does that bother us so much? Why do we need their approval so badly? It might bother us if we do make a mistake or take a misstep. But if we did something we liked, or acted our true way, why would we allow our feelings to be jeopardized? We've been trained somehow to worry about what others think about us and that's not good. When we all believe in ourselves, we cause great change in the world. Don't forget to teach what you learn."

She continues, with words that feel so transformative it's as if I'm receiving a mind transplant: "When you start thinking with your heart instead of your head, you become the best version of you, because it's the real you. Unfortunately, many people don't yet know who they are and don't realize that they are not even acting as their true self. Some will call that ego and that's, as you now know, an experience of its own. Now you say, of course, that we need our head, brain or mind to think and that the ego is created to protect us... and for a while that works. But sooner than you realize you will find that there is nothing to protect yourself *from*.

"Love, love, true love is not really known by many. But it's coming back like a big sensation and all people are ready to look at it again. They are tired and they want change.

"Tell your readers they've been asked to help with that change because they are reading this book. Everything I say is the exact expression of what I have come to know and I will tell you: it works if you surrender to it. Surrender to whom, to what?? Guess what? It only means to surrender to yourself."

Thinking about it now, I know I have not written anything that has not been said before. I am sure there are millions of books on these subjects as well. This is not something new, innovative or trendy. It's inherently older than all of us. But we've never really been taught how to do it. We never learned how to love in school. We're told to like, but not taught to love. We don't actually learn this at home either, although we have experienced it there some times. We certainly don't learn this at work. Where would we have the opportunity to learn it so deeply? We have tried our very best to mimic how we see others trying to love and hope that it is close. But ultimately, after all the major developments in the world, we still don't truthfully know love, so how could we possibly teach our children?

Chapter 9

be.come

On any given day or in any moment you should be able to give love, no matter what the situation is. That's when you know that you have started to relearn how to love. You have to start with yourself first, and then, and only then, can you move on to others. You can love anyone after you love yourself, because loving yourself is the hardest part.

Grandma, who has been patiently listening to my thoughts, says, "Here on the other side, all is well. But over there it's a big wave and a lottery of emotions. People don't know when, how or why to use the power of true love, so how could they possibly teach their children?

"This is something that has never been done before. You have never been asked to learn how to love. You thought you already knew and some of your readers may have thought they understood how to give it out. But maybe they can't receive it back. Well, defining the threads and weaving them together in this new perspective is the only way. Sisters, brothers, mothers, fathers all are required to do it. It's collective universal timing and energy for the entirety of the world. Who will choose it and who won't? It will eventually be very apparent who did and who didn't. It's one of those things that you can't excuse yourself from. It's for the fat, short, tall, skinny, funny, bald and the super hairy people too," she laughs. "It's also for executives, bosses, janitors, rich and poor alike. It's for men, for women. And it's your job to show the children.

"You are not perfect, Birdie. There is no such thing. You have learned so much but will continue to make mistakes in order to grow. There is no such thing as perfect and no such thing as staying the same. Others will come with you on this path, but it's about you going first. If you have never gone first, don't despair because there is *actually* no such thing as *first*. You are simply being the first follower with me; I am going with you right now because that's what we were asked to do. So thank you for joining me, Birdie, and letting me be *me* with you.

"You made it safe for me to come without even realizing you were creating that situation. That's the thing about creation: we don't even know that we do it. We create every single thing in our lives and then sometimes we are shocked at the results or even dislike the results, but if we had created it differently by taking different steps or making different choices, that result would have looked entirely different. But you know that. You just forget to practice it sometimes. So practice creating you the way you really want.

"Love and let others love," she concludes.

"To be loved you have to give love to others.
You get what you give.
You keep what you are.
If you want abundance, you have to create it by asking for it with love.
If you listen to your feelings, you will be healthier and make better decisions.
When your higher self talks, listen.
When you see wrong, make it right.
Love changes everything.
Love will change the world."

Chapter 9

Every once in a while I get stumped and so I bow my head and ask the Creator, "What do I need to know? What do you want me to tell them?"

In this moment, I do just that and the Creator says, "Write that down," so I do.

I am just doing what I am told to do with this entire book by giving you what I am getting. I *feel* like this is not a book I would have ever written, mostly because I *never* wanted to write a book. So I am allowing it to flow *through* me, just as I have from the start.

Four years ago, I had this dream where I was in a white bi-level house that was located right beside a hospital on 111th Avenue in Dawson Creek. In the dream, I walked in the front door and up the stairs. It felt as though there was a party or something going on in the house. It felt good and fun.

Satin sheets lay all over the floor and were slightly blowing around from a gentle wind in the room. The sheets took up most of the floor space and as I walked up the steps I had to step on them. But I *felt* like they were royal somehow. I knew they were important sheets and was hopping along trying really hard not to wrinkle them. I kept saying, "Sorry, sorry." There was a man there, leaning against the wall. He was an older man. He looked gentle and smart. He looked me in the eye and said, "Don't worry, don't apologize, it's time for me to step aside so you can do your work."

I didn't know what to say back to him. I wondered, "What work?" I woke up shortly afterward, knowing that the man in the dream was God.

I dreamed this dream a few years before I started the process of this book. Is my imagination so overactive that I would create dreams like that? Or could that have been intuition telling me to write this book for all the people who would one day read it? I don't know, but regardless, it's all part of the universal collective. I have had a few more dreams like that; not exactly the same, but all had similar messages.

Like the last dream. A dream I had a few weeks ago. The dream that felt like Grandma's message to me about what the rest of my life would feel like, as I continually be.come my true self.

I was standing beside the white picket fence in my yard on Bear Mountain. The forest was fragrant and the setting appeared very northern Canadian, with lots of poplar and evergreen trees. The season appeared to be early fall.

There, in the dream, was my beautiful grandma, still so small and tiny. She stood right beside the fence with me. She was wearing her usual pressed blouse and pants, but this time she felt so much more confident and knowing. Like a sensei.

Off to the far right, about 25 feet away, a group of children and a teacher stood in what appeared to be a schoolyard. I didn't *feel* they were connected to me at all. I noticed a girl with wild, bright orange hair, about age twelve. She stared at me. In fact, they all started staring at me and appeared to be judging me for being different than they were. Somehow I knew that whatever I was going to do, it was not going to be something they would understand.

Grandma signaled me to go closer to the fence. Her face was serious and her focus was specific. She looked me in the eye and nodded her head that I should go now. At that moment I knew it was time for me to step up and do something big. I had absolutely no idea where it would all go, so I kept looking at Grandma intently.

She gestured for me to lean on the top rung of the wooden fence. Confused, I lay my stomach ever so slightly on the fence and looked to her for approval. She nodded and gestured for me to continue on. I got the feeling that I was supposed to flap my arms like bird wings. It seemed silly, but again I looked to Grandma for approval. Once again she nodded.

I got started. I had to use great focus to balance my body on the fence. Like a bird I started to wave my arms in a flapping motion. Grandma watched me do what she asked and I felt that she was committed to holding space for me. We made eye contact and both acknowledged that I was on the right track.

Out of nowhere, the little redheaded girl screamed out in a wretched, annoying, high pitched voice, "Oh my God! What is she doing? She looks like a **CHICKEN**!" I was being judged and Grandma and I both knew it. I started to lose my balance and focus.

Grandma firmly signaled me to ignore her and to carry on. I started to flap harder and harder but I was still so unsure of what was going on. After a few moments, I looked down at the ground to see that I had lifted off the fence about twelve inches. I worked extremely hard, flapping intensely to stay afloat in the air. I looked over to Grandma and she smiled proudly to confirm that I had accomplished her task.

I floated back down to the fence, and stepped onto the ground. I felt ecstatic and proud of myself for learning to fly. I glanced over to the schoolyard and saw the stunned faces on all the students and the teacher; their jaws had dropped. They couldn't believe their eyes. When I looked back to Grandma, she nodded one last time, an affirmation that I could actually do what seemed impossible to others. And now I knew that they could do it too.

"See your wings, feel love and fly."

~Tryna Gower~

Notes

Notes

Notes

ABOUT THE AUTHOR

Cree-Métis spiritual warrior and award-winning entrepreneur Tryna Gower shares her story and offers inspiration through an international group she founded in 2014 called be.real. Tryna was born into a multi-cultural family with Cree, Métis, Irish, Polish and Czechoslovakian roots. Growing up in a primarily white household, she always felt different from the people she knew as her family. But her grandmother Adel Spacil (formerly Big Charles) showed her the true meaning of unconditional love through a relationship that didn't end with death.

Beyond the grave, her grandmother continued to guide her back to her aboriginal roots, and even channeled be.come, a book with a special message for humanity, through Tryna. Born in British Columbia, Canada, Tryna is grateful for the connection she feels with her homeland and the vibration of her ancestors. She loves inspiring others to be.come their true selves by developing their own intuitive and leadership gifts. Follow Tryna Gower at www.trynagower.com.

Made in the USA
Charleston, SC
09 November 2016